4

THE LOST SHEEP FOUND

by

LAURENCE CLARKSON

Published by *The Rota* at the University of Exeter
1974

04356001

ISBN 0 9501950 7 3

Reprinted in 1981 by
Short Run Press Ltd, Exeter, Great Britain

In *The lost sheep found*, Laurence Clarkson (or Claxton) records his pilgrimage through the 'Seven Churches' of mid-seventeenth century England to his rest as the only true bishop under the new third Commission to John Reeve, successor to Moses and Paul.

Born in 1615 in Preston, Lancashire, Clarkson was educated in the Church of England but became such a puritan that he secretly sought godly ministers and scrupled at asking his father's blessing (pp. 4–5). Having learned to pray *ex tempore*, he became a Presbyterian and moved to London. There he soon turned Independent and then Antinomian. In pursuit of that dispensation, he joined Col. Fleetwood's regiment in the New Model Army. Soon he was established as a preacher at Pulham Market ('Pulom') in Norfolk where he preached free grace. After about six months he turned Baptist and on November 6, 1644, was dipped 'in the water that runneth about the *Tower*' (p. 12). Returning to East Anglia he married, by mutual consent before the congregation, Robert Marchant's daughter Frances for whom he provided even during his later ramblings. He exercised his new ministry until January 24, 1644/5 when he was apprehended, as was Hanserd Knollys, on a parliamentary warrant, closely interrogated and confined at Bury St. Edmunds. By July, Clarkson had come under the influence of William Erbery: 'So finding I was but still in *Egypt* burning Brick, I was minded to travel into the Wilderness; so seeing the vanity of the Baptists, I renounced them and had my freedom' (p. 19). Thus Clarkson turned Seeker and wrote his first work *The pilgrimage of saints, by church cast out, in Christ found, seeking truth* (London, 1646). He came to Thomas Edwards's notice, who confirms Clarkson's claim (p. 23) that he preached at Bow Church, see *Gangraena* (1st ed. London, 1646), part ii, pp. 7–8. For a year, Clarkson held a ministry at Sandridge in Hertfordshire. Having been turned out he became an itinerant preacher and wrote for a fee of twelve pounds, *A generall charge or, impeachment of high-treason in the name of Justice Equity, against the communality of England* (London, 1647). This pamphlet has a levelling tone: the communality is acused of a number of serious offences by the messenger of Justice-Equity, Experienced Reason, who replies to the communality's objections to the charges. Experienced Reason castigates the communality for choosing oppressors to represent them 'for who are the oppressors, but the Nobility and Gentry; and who are the oppressed, is not the Yeoman, the Farmer, the Tradesman, and the Labourer?' (p. 11). Experienced Reason insists that this is a consequence of allowing the franchise to be confined to freeholders and freemen of corporations. Experienced Reason does not hesitate to condemn unequal taxation, social privilege, lawyers, clerics, the excise, justices of the peace, press censorship, tithes and the directory of worship.

Having wearied of the small parish in Lincolnshire to which he was next presented, Clarkson rejoined the army as teacher to Captain Cambridge's company. Being given two month's leave, he visited his wife before rejoining his regiment in London. There, through Giles Calvert, the radical publisher, he contacted 'a people called *My one flesh*' (p. 24). Clarkson thus turned Ranter and wrote *A single eye, all light, no darkness* (London, 1650). (Excerpts from this tract may be found in N. Cohn, *The pursuit of the millenium* [London, 1957], pp. 347–53.) At this time, Clarkson was an extreme antinomian who held 'that no man could be free'd from sin, till he had acted that so called sin, as no sin' (p. 25). As 'Captain of the Rant', Clarkson indulged in a licentious, roving life and even counted Major William Rainborough among his acquaintances. Arrested under a parliamentary warrant, and examined by a committee of the Rump, Clarkson was imprisoned for blasphemy and his book burnt, but the further sentence of banishment was not executed; Rainborough was disabled from being a justice of the peace (*C.J.*, 27 Sept. 1650, VI, 474–75). When released Clarkson added the practice of astrology, healing and magic to his ranting. At last, called in 1658 to Faith as opposed to the various dispensations of Reason, this world and the devil, he published several works in justification of his new position, culminating with *The lost sheep found* which ends with an attack on the Quakers and the assertion of the true third Commission of John Reeve. Ludowick Muggleton, with whom Clarkson was at odds, is never mentioned. However in 1661, Clarkson submitted to Muggleton and was received into favour. Clarkson died in 1667, a prisoner for debt in Ludgate; he had lent a hundred pounds to help rebuild after London's great fire but the borrowers absconded.

Details of Clarkson's life are noted in *D.N.B.*; his life and doctrines are more extensively discussed by A. L. Morton in *The world of the ranters* (London, 1970), pp. 115–42, which quotes several pages of *The lost sheep found* as well as a number of other documents; Clarkson is briefly mentioned in P. Zagorin, *A history of political thought in the English revolution* (London, 1954), pp. 31–32 which advocates reprinting the present work; and his life and views are used by C. Hill, in *The world turned upside down* (London, 1972), see esp. pp. 171–74, 254–56.

The lost sheep found, Wing C4580, British Library shelf mark 1352. c. 38, is reproduced by permission of the Board of the British Library.

The Loſt ſheep

FOUND:

OR,

The Prodigal returned to his Fathers
houſe, after many a ſad and weary
Journey through many Religious Countreys,

Where now, notwithſtanding all his former Tranſgreſſions, and breach of his Fathers Commands,
he is received in an eternal Favor, and all the
righteous and wicked Sons that he hath left behinde, reſerved for eternal miſery ;

As all along every Church or Diſpenſation may
read in his Travels, their Portion after
this Life.

Written by Laur. Claxton, *the onely true converted
Meſſenger of Chriſt Jeſus, Creator of
Heaven and Earth.*

LONDON:

Printed for the Author. 1660.

The Loſt ſheep
FOUND:
OR,
The Prodigal returned to his Fathers houſe, after many a ſad and weary Journey through many religious Countreys.

Aving publiſhed ſeveral Writings in confirmation of this ſpiritual laſt Commiſſion that ever ſhall appear in this unbelieving World , a Well-wiſher to this Commiſſion, yea a man of no mean parts nor Parentage in this Reaſons kingdom, much importuned me to publiſh to this periſhing world, the various leadings forth of my ſpirit through each Diſpenſation , from the year 1630, to this year 1660. and that for no other end , than that Reaſon, or the Devils mouth might be ſtopped , with the hypocriſie of his heart laid naked, and the tongues of Faith with praiſes opened, to conſider what variety of By-paths , and multiplicity of ſeeming realities, yet abſolute notions, the ſouls of the Elect may wander or travel through, ſeeking reſt, and yet find none till the day unexpected , that Soul as a brand be plucked out of the fire of his own righteouſneſs, or profeſſed wickedneſs, unto the true belief of a real Commiſſion which quencheth all the fiery darts of ſin, that Diſpenſations have left cankering in his ſoul, [minde this] as have but patience , and thou ſhalt hear the more. I labored for perfect cure and peace in my ſoul,

the

the further I was from it, infomuch that I was refolved to feek forth no more, fuppofing my felf in as perfect health and liberty in my fpirit, as any then profefsing an unknown God whatfoever.

As do but ferioufly minde this en uing Epiftle, and thou mayeft in me read thy own hypocrifie and diffimulation in point of Worfhip all along; as in that year 16 0. being of the Age of fifteen yeares, and living with my Parents in the town of *Prefton* in *Amounderneſs*, where I was born, and educated in the Form and Worfhip of the Church of *England*, then eſtabliſhed in the Title of the *Epifcopal*, or Biſhops Government; then, and in that year, my heart began to enquire after the pureſt Miniſtery held forth under that Form, not being altogether void of fome fmall difcerning, who preached Chriſt more truly and powerfully, as I thought, than another, and unto them was I onely refolved to follow their Doctrine above any other, and to that end my brethren being more gifted in the knowledge of the Scriptures than my felf, and very zealous in what they knew, that they did often prevail with Mr. *Hudſon* our Town-Lecturer, to admit of fuch Miniſters as we judged were true laborious Miniſters of Chriſt, who when they came, would thunder againſt Superſtition, and ſharply reprove Sin, and prophaning the Lords-day; which to hear, tears would run down my cheeks for joy: fo having a pitiful fuperſtitious fellow the Miniſter of our Town, I fpared no pains to travel to *Standiſh* and other places, where we could hear of a Godly Miniſter, as feveral times I have gone ten miles, more or lefs, faſting all the day, when my Parents never knew of it, and though I have been weary and hungry, yet I came home rejoycing. Then the Miniſters had an Order, that none ſhould receive the Sacrament, but fuch as would take it at the rayled Altar kneeling, which I could not do, and therefore went to fuch Miniſters in the Countrey that gave it fitting: Now a while after Mr. *Starby* the Miniſter of our Town, taking notice of feaving our Pariſh, informed our father the danger of his children going into Hereſie, and the trouble that

would

would enſue upon our father and his children, beſides the
diſgrace of all good Church-men, which did much incenſe our
father, but all to no purpoſe, for I thought it conſcience to
obey God before man; however I being under my fathers
tuition, he caſt a ſtrict eye over me, and would force me to
read over the prayers in the book of *Common-prayer* and *Practice of Piety*, which I have done, till they have fallen aſleep
and my ſelf, this was our devotion in thoſe days; but increaſing
in knowledge, I judged to pray another mans form, was vaine
babling, and not acceptable to God : and then the next thing
I ſcrupled, was asking my parents bleſſing, that often times
in the winter mornings, after I have been out of my bed, I
have ſtood freezing above, and durſt not come down till my
father was gone abroad, and the reaſon I was ſatisfied, the
bleſſing or prayers of a wicked man God would not hear, and
ſo ſhould offend God to ask him bleſſing ; for either of theſe
two ways I muſt, down on my knees, and ſay, Father pray to
God to bleſs me, or give me your bleſſing for Gods ſake, either
of which I durſt not uſe with my lips, but was in me refrain-
ed; and I improved my knowledge in the Doctrine of thoſe
men I judged was the true Miniſters of God, ſo that with
teares many times I have privatly ſought the Lord as I thought,
whether thoſe things that the puritanical Prieſts preached, was
my own, and the more I was troubled, that I could not pray
without a Book as my brethren did, fain would I have been
judged a Profeſſor with them, but wanted parts, yet often
times have had motions to tender my ſelf to prayer amongſt
them, but durſt not, and to that end I might be admitted to
pray with them, I have prayed alone to try how I could pray,
but could not utter my ſelf as I knew they did: ſo I remember
their was a day of Humiliation to be ſet apart by the Puritans
ſo called, to ſeek God by prayer and expounding of Scriptures,
againſt which day I took my pen, and writ a pretty form of
words, ſo got them by heart, and when the day came I was
called to improve my gifts, at which I was glad, yet in a trembling condition leſt I ſhould be foyled ; however, to Prayer I
    went,

went, with a devotion as though I had known the true God, but alas, when I was in the midst of that Prayer, I lost my form of words, and so was all in a sweat as though I had been sick, and so came off like a hypocrite as I was, which so seized on my soul, that I thought for my hypocrisie damnation would be my portion; however it humbled me, that I was glad to become one of the meanest of the number, still full of fears that when I died, I should go to hell ; in which time I writ all the hypocrisie of my heart in a Letter to send to Mr. *Hudson* our Lecturer, to know his judgement whether such a soul as there related might be saved ? in the interim comes a motion within me, saying, *A fool, why dost thou send to man that knows not what will become of his own soul? burn it, and wait upon me* ; which Letter I did burn, and not many weeks after I had a gift of Prayer that was not inferior to my brethren, for which I was glad for the goodness of God to my soul ; and as I increased in knowledge, so was my zeal, that I have many times privately prayed with rough hard Sinders under my bare knees, that so God might hear me ; and when I could not end my Prayers with tears running down my cheeks, I was afraid some sin shut the attention of God from me : and thus did I do for a few years, in which time the Bishops began to totter and shake, yea, for their cruelty and superstition, was totally routed.

Now if then you had asked me what I thought God was, the Devil was, what the Angels nature was, what Heaven and Hell was, and what would become of my soul after death?

My answer had plainly bin this : That my God was a grave, ancient, holy, old man, as I supposed sat in Heaven in a chair of gold, but as for his nature I knew no more than a childe : and as for the Devil, I really believed was some deformed person out of man, and that he could where, when, and how, in what shape appear he pleased; and therefore the devil was a great Scar-croe, in so much that every black thing I saw in the night, I thought was the devil : But as for the Angels, I knew nothing at all ; and for Heaven I thought was a glorious place,

with

with variety of rooms suitable for Himself, and his Son Chrift, and the Holy Ghoft : and Hell, where it was I knew not, but judged it a local place, all dark, fire and brimftone, which the devils did torment the wicked in, and that for ever ; but for the foul at the hour of death, I believed was either by an Angel or a Devil fetcht immediately to Heaven or Hell. This was the height of my knowledge under the Bifhops Government, and I am perfwaded was the height of all Epifcopal Minifters then living ; fo that furely if they fhall be eftablifhed for a National Miniftery , they will not impofe fuch Ceremonies as then they did, but are grown wifer about God and Devil ; for they will finde the major part of *England* is grown wifer, fo cannot ftoop to an inferiour Light ; therefore if ye now begin to ftand, take heed left ye fall.

Secondly, After this I travelled into the Church of the Presbyterians, where ftill I made Brick of ftraw and clay , nay there I found my foul the more oppreffed, and further enfnared in the land of *Egypt* , burning Brick all the day ; but I knowing no further light, I was willing to bear their yoke, and fometimes found it pleafant ; for herein confifted the difference of the Presbyterian and Epifcopal , onely in a few fuperfititious Rites and Ceremonies, as alfo their Doctrine was more lively than the Epifcopal , for they would thunder the Pulpit with an unknown God , which then I thought was true, and fharply reprove fin , though fince I faw we were the greateft finners ; but however their Doctrine I liked, it being the higheft I then heard of : So war being begun betwixt the Epifcopal and the Presbyterian, I came for *London* , where I found them more precife than in our Popifh Countrey of *Lancafhire* ; for with us the Lords-day was highly profaned by the toleration of May-poles, Dancing and Rioting , which the Presbyterians hated, and in their Doctrine cryed out againft , which thing my foul alfo hated , though yet I was not clear but the Steeple was the houfe of God , from that faying of *David*, Pfalm 84.10. faying, *For a day in thy Courts is better than a thoufand : I had rather be a Door-keeper in the houfe of my God,*
                                                                    than

than to dwell in the tents of wickedness; so that I finding out the ablest Teachers in *London*, as then I judged was Mr. *Calamy*, *Case*, *Brooks*, and such like, unto whom I daily resorted, if possible, to get assurance of Salvation, not neglecting to receive the Ordinance of Breaking of Bread from them, judging in so doing, *I shewed forth the Lords death till he came.* Now the persecution of the Bishops fell so heavy upon the Presbyterian Ministers, that some fled for *New-England*; and *Hooker* had left several Books in print, which so tormented my soul, that I thought it unpossible to be saved; however, I labored what in me lay, to finde those signs and marks in my own soul, and to that end neglected all things that might hinder it; and thus for a certain time I remained a hearer of them, till such time that Wars began to be hot, and they pressed the people to send out their husbands and servants to help the Lord against the Mighty, by which many a poor soul knowing no better, was murthered, and murthered others, taking the Bible in their Pockets, and the Covenant in their Hats, by me was esteemed the work and command of the Lord, not at all minding the command of the second Commission to the contrary, as in 2 *Cor.* 10. 4. saying, *We do not war after the flesh, for the weapons of our warfare are not carnal, but mighty through God to the pulling down of strong holds,* &c. This was not by me understood, but as they did in the old time in *Moses* his Commission, so I thought we might do then; in which time the Presbyterians began to be a great people, and in high esteem, and at that time there was a great slaughter of the Protestants in *Ireland*, that *London* was thronged with their Ministers and people, and several Collections was gathered for them: but this I observed, that as the Presbyterians got power, so their pride and cruelty increased against such as was contrary to them, so that

Thirdly I left them, and travelled to the Church of the Independents; for this I observed as wars increased, so variety of Judgements increased: and coming to them, of which was Mr. *Goodwin*, and some others, I discerned their Doctrine
clearer,

clearer, and of a more moderate spirit: Now the greatest difference betwixt them, was about baptizing of infants, pleading by Scripture, that none but the infants or children of Believers ought to be baptized; and that none of them must receive the Sacrament, as then it was called, but such as was Church-members, judging all that was not congregated into fellowship, were not of God, but the world: So that about these things I was searching the truth thereof, and labored in the letter of the Scripture to satisfie my judgement; in the interim hearing of one Doctor *Crisp*, to him I went, and he held forth against all the aforesaid Churches, That let his people be in society or no, thorgh walked all alone, yet if he believed that Christ Jesus died for him, God beheld no iniquity in him: and to that end I serioufly perused his Bookes, and found it proved by Scripture, as it is written *Numbers* 23. 21. *He hath not beheld iniquity in* Jacob, *neither hath he seen perverfeness in* Israel. This was confirmed by other Scriptures, that I conceived whose sins Christ died for, their sin was to be required no more; for thus thinking when the debt was paid, the Creditor would not look upon him as indebted to him, yet this I ever thought Christ never died for all, though the Scripture was fluent to that purpose, yet I found Scriptures to the contrary, and was ever as touching that satisfied, that as Christ prayed for none but such as was given him out of the world, *I pray for them, I pray not for the world*, so that I thought he did not die for them he would not pray for, which thought now I know is true, and have by pen, and can by tongue make good the same: But I must return to the time then under Doctor *Crisp*'s Doctrine, in which I did endeavor to become one of those that God saw no sin, and in some measure I began to be comforted therewith, but how, or which way to continue in the same I could not tell; having as yet but little understanding in the Scripture I was silent, onely still enquiring after the highest pitch of Light then held forth in *London*, in which time Mr. *Randel* appeared, with Mr. *Simpson*, with such a Doctrine as Doctor *Crisp*, onely higher and clearer, which then was

called

called *Antinomians*, or againſt the Law, ſo that I left all Church-fellowſhip, and burning of Brick in *Egypt*, and travelled with them up and down the borders, part *Egypt*, and part Wilderneſs.

Fourthly, take notice in this Sect I continued a certain time, for Church it was none, in that it was but part form, and part none; in which progreſs I had a great ſort of profeſſors acquainted with me, ſo begin to be ſome body amongſt them, and having a notable gift in Prayer, we often aſſembled in private, improving my gifts, judging then the beſt things of this world was onely prepared for the ſaints, of which then I judged my ſelf one, not knowing any other but that God was a Spirit, and did motion in and out into his Saints, and that this was Gods Kingdom, and we his people; and therefore I judged God did fight for us againſt our enemies, that ſo we might enjoy him in liberty : At which time *Paul Hobſon* brake forth with ſuch expreſſions of the in-comes and out-goes of God, that my ſoul much deſired ſuch a gift of preaching, which after a while *Hobſon* and I being acquainted, he had a Captains place under Colonel *Fleetwood* for *Yarmouth*, ſo that thither with him I went, and there tarried a ſoldier with them, at which time I had a ſmall gift of Preaching, and ſo by degrees increaſed into a method, that I attempted the Pulpit at Mr. *Wardels* Pariſh in *Suffolk*, and ſo acquainted my gifts more and more in publick, that having got acquaintance at *Norwich*, I left the Company at *Yarmouth*; ſo after a few dayes I was admitted into a Pulpit two or three times : ſo coming a man from *Pulom* ſide in *Norfolk* and hearing of me, was greatly affected with my Doctrine, but eſpecially my Prayer, and was very urgent with me to go to their Pariſh of *Ruſſel*. which within two weeks after I aſſented to be there ſuch a day, which was againſt the Faſt-day; for at that time the Parliament had eſtabliſhed a Monethly Faſt, which was the laſt wedneſday of the moneth : at the ſet time I came to the place appointed, where this man had given notice to the beſt affected people in thoſe parts, what a rare man was to preach that day, which thing I
was

was ambitious of, as also to get some silver: Well, to the matter I went, and as was my Doctrine, so was their understanding, though I say't, as young as I was, yet was not I inferior
to any Priest in those days : So in conclusion of my days work
there came several in the Church-yard to me, and gave me
thanks for my paines, yea, hoped the Lord would settle me
among them, which news I was glad to hear ; so for the next
Lords-Day by Goodman *Mays* and *Burton* was I invited to
preach at *Pulom*, which was a great Parish ; so upon liking I
went, and was well approved of by all the Godly, so there
for a time I was settled for twenty shillings a week, and very
gallantly was provided for, so that I thought I was in Heaven
upon earth judging the Priests had a brave time in this world,
to have a house built for them, and means provided for them,
to tell the people stories of other mens works. Now after I
had continued half a year, more or less, the Ministers began
to envy me for my Doctrine, it being free Grace, so contrary to theirs, and that the more, their people came from their
own Parish to hear me, so that they called me *Sheep-stealer*
for robbing them of their flock, and to that end came to catch
and trap me at several Lectures where I was called, that at
last they prevailed with the Heads of the Parish to turn me
out, so I slighting them as they could me, we parted, and then
having many friends, I was importuned to come and live with
them, so above all I chose *Robert Marchants* house my Lodging
place, because his Daughter I loved ; and for a certain time
preached up and down in several Churches, both of *Suffolk*
and *Norfolk*, and many times in private, that I had a great
company. Now in the interim there was one *John Tyler* a
Colchester man frequented those parts where then I inhabited,
who was a Teacher of the Baptists, and had a few scattered
up and down the Countrey, which several times we had meetings and converse about a lawful Minister: now I knowing no
other but that those sayings, *Go ye teach all Nations, baptizing
them, and lo I am with you to the end of the world* ; that conti-
nuance to the end of the world, was the Load-stone that

brought

brought me to believe that the Baptism of the Apostles was as much in force now, as in their days, and that Command did as really belong to me as to them; so being convinced, for *London* I went to be further satisfied, so that after a little discourse with *Patience*, I was by him baptized in the water that runneth about the *Tower*, after which I stayed at *London* about a week.

Fifthly, then for *Suffolk* again I travelled through the Church of the Baptists, and was of *Robert Marchants* family received with joy, for I had the love of all the family; and though he had four Daughters marriageable, yet there was one I loved above any in that Countrey, though I was beloved of other friends daughters far beyond her in estate, yet for her knowledge and moderation in spirit, I loved her; so there up and down a certain time I continued preaching the Gospel, and very zealous I was for obedience to the Commands of Christ Jesus; which Doctrine of mine converted many of my former friends and others, to be baptized, and so into a Church-fellowship was gathered to officiate the order of the Apostles, so that really I thought if ever I was in a true happy condition, then I was, knowing no other but as aforesaid, that this Command of Christ did as really belong to me as to them; and we having the very same rule, as Elders and Deacons, with Dipping, and Breaking of bread in the same manner as they, I was satisfied we onely were the Church of Christ in this world.

Thus having a great company, and baptizing of many into that Faith, there was no small stir among the priests what to do with me, which afterwards they got a Warrant from the Parliament, to apprehend Mr. *Knowles* and my self, for then *Knowles* was about *Ipswich* preaching that doctrine, and baptizing certain people into that Faith; now they apprehended Mr. *Knowls* in *Ipswich* Goal, and from thence with their Warrant came to secure me, so in the week day being privately assembled in a friends house, within three miles of *Ay*, there came in an Officer from the Parliament with certain Soldiers,

and

and two Conftables, with fome of the parifh, having clubs and ftaves furrounded the houfe, I being earneft in my doctrine, and at that time was very much preffing the people, that without fubmitting to Baptifm all their profeffion was nothing, proving by Scripture that as Chrift was our patern, fo we muft follow him as enfample, which could not be unlefs we kept his commandments, as it is written, *If ye love me, keep my commandments* : Now dipping being a command of Chrift, I judged them rebells that did profefs the name of Chrift, and not fubmit their bodies to the Ordinance of Chrift, and that Chrift requires obedience from none but fuch as was capaple of being taught, and therefore no children, but men and women, ought to receive the Ordinance of Baptifm, in which time fome of the Officers hearing me, interrupted me in my doctrine, and told me I muft leave off, and go along with them, fhewing me the Authority they had from the Parliament ; however, fome of our friends would have oppofed them, but I faw it was in vain, and fo defired our friends to be quiet, and faid, we muft not onely profefs Chrift, but alfo fuffer for him ; fo it being in the winter time, and almoft night, they hafted me for *Ay*, though I, with our friends, defired but fo much liberty as to go to my wifes fathers houfe for linnen and other neceffaries, and they would engage for my appearance before the Committee at *Bury* ; but all in vain, then my wife told them they fhould provide a horfe for her, for whither ever I went, fhe would go : at which they were very much incenfed, but all to no purpofe, fo at laft a Trooper would have her to ride behind him, but fhe with fcorn refufed, then they got her furniture to ride behind me, fo taking leave with our friends, to *Ay* that night we were carried; now one of them went before to provide Lodging, fo the Town having intelligence they had taken a great Anabaptift, there was no fmall waiting for my coming, that when I came into the entering of the town, the inhabitants had befet both fides of the ftreets to fee my perfon, fuppofing an Anabaptift had bin a ftrange creature, but when they beheld me, with my wife, they faid one to another, He is like one of us, yea, they are a very pretty couple, it is pity I fhould
fuffer :

suffer : so to the Inne I came , where a great company was in the yard to behold me ; so being unnoticed , they guarded me to our Lodging , and great provision was made for Supper, where many a pot was spent that night to see my face ; so to bed we went , and in the next room by Soldiers guarded, so in the morning we were halted for *St. Edmonds Bury* , which that morning Captain *Harvey* give out many sad and grievous words what the Committee would do with me , but the devil was deceived ; however I said little : so they came to me with a Bill what I had to pay for Beer, Wine, and Meat; unto which I said, I had none , but if I had , I would pay none, it was sufficient I was wrongfully deprived of my freedom, and not to pay for their rioting ; however they told me, I must before I go ; then keep me here still : surely, said I , your Masters that set you on work, are able to pay you your Wages : Well , they said before I came out of prison , if I were not hanged, I should pay it ; then said I, rest your selves contented till that day : so towards *Bury* we took our Journey, and one was gone before to inform the Committee I was taken ; against my appearance they were assembled in a full Committee, of which as I take it , Captain *Bloyes* of *Woodbridge* was then Chair-man. So to the Hall I was guarded, the room being full, I was conveyed up to the Chair-man, who asked my name ? To which I replied, this was strange that you had a Warrant to take me , and know not my name : Well , that was no matter, do you tell us your name ; so I told them : What countrey-man are you ? I said *Lancashire*. What made you travel so far off into these parts ? The like motions that moved others, moved me. How long have you professed this way of dipping ? Not so long as I ought to have done, had my understanding been enlightened. What then , you approve of what you do ? Otherways I should not do it. How many have you dipped in these parts ? I being a free born subject of this Nation ought not to accuse my self ; but you are to prove your charge , by sufficient witness against me ; but however I being brought before you for my obedience to the Commands of

of Christ, I am neither afraid nor ashamed to tell you what I
have done : but to give you an account how many I have dipped , that I cannot tell. Then you have dipped some ? Yea,
that I have. After what manner do you dip them ? After a
decent order. We are informed you dip both men and women
naked ? As unto that you are not rightly informed. Where is
your *Jordan* you dip them in ? Though it is not *Jordan* , yet
there are several places convenient. Do you not dip them
in the night ? Yea. And why do you not dip them in the day,
it being an Ordinance of Christ as you say ? Because such as
you are not able to bear the truth. Then said Sir *William
Spring* but Mr. *Claxton*, have not you forced some in the water
against their will? That is contrary to Scripture. Did you not
one time, being on horf-back, with a switch force some into the
wate ? Let them that so informed you, affirm it before you
to my face. But Mr. *Claxton* who were those that you dipped
about *Framingham* ? At this time I cannot remember, but several I have dipped there aways. Did not you dip six Sisters
there about at one time ? I never dipped six at one time.
Then said Sir *John Rowse*, we are informed you dipped six Sisters one night naked. That is nothing to me what you are informed, for I never did such a thing ; Nay further, it is repor-
ted, that which of them you liked best, you lay with her in the
water? Surely your experience teacheth you the contrary, that
nature hath small desire to copulation in water, at which they
laughed; But, said I, you have more cause to weep for the unclean thoughts of your heart. Mr. *Claxton* have not you a
wife? One that brought me, said she is in town. Where is she?
Fetch her hither : she being without the door, came in quickly,
and took me by the hand. Well, said the Chair-man, you are a
loving woman, is this your husband ? Yes , he is my husband.
How long have you been married ? About two moneths.
Where were you married ? At *Waybread* in my fathers house.
Who married you ? My husband, with the consent of my
parents, and the Church. At that there was a great laughter,
and said, your husband marry you to himself, that is against the
law,

law; I being vexed at their folly, answered, Marriage is no other, but a free consent in love each to the other before God, and who was sufficient to publish the Contract as my self? Nay but Mr. *Claxton*, you are not rightly informed as touching a true Marriage. I say I was married according to truth: then if your Marriage be lawful, we are not lawfully married. I question not yours, look ye to that; but this I know, and can prove, I am married according to the word of God; neither can your law repeal the contract of that couple, that hath their parents consent, and the Church confirming the same. Well, well, we shall give you the hearing, but how many was present when you took her to your wife? About twelve. What did you say to her and the Church? First, I sought the Lord by prayer for a blessing upon that Ordinance, and then I declared unto her parents and the Church what had passed betwixt she and I, and that before them all I took her by the hand, and asked her if she was not willing to take me for her husband during life? To which she assented, as also her parents approved of it, and gave her to me with the confirmation of the Church. Then said the Chair-man, What think you Gentlemen, of this Marriage? They said it was a strange Marriage. What then Mrs. *Claxton*, you look upon this man your lawful husband? Yea, I deny all other men in the world. Then you have lain with him? I ought to ly with no other. But Mrs. *Claxton*, did your husband dip you before, or after he became your husband? Before I was contracted in publick? How or after what manner did your husband dip you? in your clothes or naked? Sir, we defie any undecent carriage, if you were dipped in your clothes you would spoil them, and besides it might endanger your life with cold: we have clothes for both men and women provided for that purpose. What were you plunged over head and ears? So saith the Scripture. What Mr. *Claxton*, did you go with her into the water? No I stood on the bank side. Mrs. *Claxton*, were not you amazed, or almost drowned? No Sir, the obedience to the Command of God did shut out all fear and cold. What did not you go to bed

after

after dipped? I had a warm bed with dry linnen provided? Did not your husband lodge with you that night? There is no such wickedness among us. Why what matter, you were married before God. Till we were publickly before witness, we had no such custom, and let me tell you, if it be the practise of your Church, it is not so in ours. Nay woman, be not angry, I do not say you did so, for truly I am as much against sin as you are. But Mrs. *Claxton*, we have an Order to secure your husband, and there to endure the pleasure of the Parliament, what will you do? we have no Order to stay you. If you stay my husband, you must stay me also. Why, are you willing to go to Goal with your husband? For the cause of Christ I am willing to suffer imprisonment. Then you are resolved yours is the way of Truth. Then said I, for the present I know no Truth but this. Well Mr. *Claxton*, after a while you will be otherwise informed. Never to turn back again. We are to commit you to custody, that so you may seduce no more people. Sir, I must obey your pleasure, but I shall not deny to be obedient to the Command of Christ. Well, we shall talk with you another time: so they ordered to make my *Mittimus*, and in my presence gave it Captain *Poe* my Keeper, and said, Mr. *Claxton*, you may take notice that the Parliament is favorable to you, that they will not send you to the common Goal, but to a house where none but men of Quality are kept in custody. Then said *Poe*, who was my Goaler, what shall his wife do? Then said my wife, Where ever my husband is, there will I be, then the Committee Ordered her with me: so coming thither, there was none but two Papists Knights, and a Sea Captain, so after we had supped, we were directed to our Chamber, which was a large chamber, and pretty good Furniture. Now under a week I told Captain *Poe* that I was not able to board at half a crown a Meal. Then, saith he, you must go to the common Goal: Thither would I go, for I am not ashamed to sit in the flocks in the Market-place, for the Name of Christ. So he informed the Committee, but they would not remove me, and said, he must agree for the cham-

C

ber,

ber, and I finde my self Diet : At this *Poe* was vexed, and
sent up his Handmaid Mistriss *Tuck*, to agree with me for the
chamber at four shillings a week, which for the space of half a
year I gave her, in which time our people increased, there being *William Muly* and some others of this way in *Bury*, I had
oftentimes money from the Army, and the Churches at *London* and *Colchester*, so that I wanted for nothing ; and some
came to my chamber, and there I preached unto them, in so
much that the Keeper informed the Committee, who that Sunday at night assembled, to consider what to do with me : in
conclusion they shut me close prisoner, and kept my wife from
me, which was more grief to me then the rest. Well, against
the next Lords-day I appointed our friends to stand before
my window on the *Argel-hill*, that being the way for all the
great Ones of the Town to go to their worship, so at the very
instant time putting my head forth of the Window, I did
boldly exhort the people to beware of the priests, and while it
is the time of your health , submit your souls and bodies in
obedience to the true Baptism , and be no longer deluded to
think that your infants are commanded to obey, or capable of
an Ordinance imposed upon them. Oh for shame, if not for
fear, stand still and hear the truth related by his true and lawful Minister, otherwise turn back again ; At which a great sort
of people gave attention, which did enrage the Priest and Magistrate, yet they knew not what to do with me , but charged
me to do so no more. Then said I, take heed how you keep
my wife from me : is this to do as you would be done unto ?
so they forthwith took off the Pad-lock, and let my friends
come to me. After this I had the liberty of the whole house,
nay, to sit at the street-door ; for he had no prisoners but
such as gave in great security for their safe imprisonment ; and
as for me, and *Westrop* my fellow-prisoner, they feared not our
going away, onely they were afraid I should dip some. So a
little after, Spring coming on, I got liberty, not being well, to
go abroad with a Keeper, and Captain *Gray* , who was called
Captain **Drink-water**, was to go with me : Now above all the
reft,

rest, I desired Captain *Gray* to go with me to a Wood a mile distant from me; it having rained over night, the Brook was up, so a man coming with a Pole, I desired him to lay it over, which he did, so I went over first, and the Captain followed me, and shaking the Pole, he fell in to the middle in water, and in a trembling condition he was, lest the Committee should hear of it; so to the Wood we went, and there he dried his Hose and Stockings, so after we came to prison again, the Committee hearing of it, questioned Captain *Gray*, but he told them the truth, at which they laughed. After I had lain there a long time, Mr. *Sedgewick*, and Mr. *Erbery* came to visit me, with whom I had great discourse, and after they were gone, I had a great contest in my minde, as touching the succession of Baptism, which I could not see but in the death of the Apostles, there was never since no true Administrator; for I could not read there was ever any that had power by imposition of hands, to give the Holy Ghost, and work miracles as they did; so that in the death of them I concluded Baptism to either young or old, was ceased. Now observe, I could discern this, but could not by the same rule see that preaching and prayer was to cease: for this now I know, as in the death of the Apostles, and them commissionated by them, the Commission ceased, as unto all their Form and Worship: So finding I was but still in *Egypt* burning Brick, I was minded to travel into the Wilderness; so seeing the vanity of the Baptists, I renounced them and had my freedom. Then

Sixthly, I took my journey into the society of those people called *Seekers*, who worshipped God onely by prayer and preaching, therefore to *Ely* I went, to look for *Sedgwick* and *Erbery* but found them not, onely their people were assembled: with whom I had discourse, but found little satisfaction; so after that for *London* I went to finde *Seekers* there, which when I came, there was divers fallen from the Baptists as I had done, so coming to *Horn* in *Fleet lane*, and *Fleten* in *Seacoul-lane*, they informed me that several had left the Church of *Patience*, in seeing the vanity of *Kiffin* and others, how highly they

took

took it upon them, and yet could not prove their Call succesfively; so glad was I there was a people to have society withal; then was I moved to put forth a book which was the first that ever I writ, bearing this Title, *The pilgrimage of Saints*, *by church cast out, in Christ found, seeking truth*, this being a sutable peece of work in those days, that it wounded the Churches; which book *Randel* owned, and sold many for me. Now as I was going over *London-bridge*, I met with *Thomas Gun* a teacher of the Baptists, who was a man of a very humble, moderate spirit, who asked me if I own'd the *Pilgrimage of Saints*? I told him yea: then said he, you have writ against the church of Christ, and have discovered your self an enemy to Christ. Then I said, it is better be a hypocrite to man then to God, for I finde as much dissimulation, covetousness, back-biting and envy, yea as filthy wickedness among some of them, as any people I know: and notwithstanding your heaven-like carriage, if all your faults were written in your forehead, for ought I know, you are a hypocrite as well as I; which afterwards it was found out he had lain with his Landlady many times; and that he might satisfie his Lust, upon slighty erands, he sent her husband into the country, that so he might lodge with his wife all night; which being found out, so smote his conscience, that he privately took a Pistol and shot himself to death in *Georges-fields*. As all along in this my travel I was subject to that sin, and yet as saint-like, as though sin were a burden to me, so that the fall of this *Gun* did so seize on my soul, that I concluded there was none could live without sin in this world; for notwithstanding I had great knowledge in the things of God, yet I found my heart was not right to what I pretended, but full of lust and vain-glory of this world, finding no truth in sincerity that I had gone through, but meerly the vain pride and conceit of Reasons imagination, finding my heart with the rest, seeking nothing but the praise of men in the heighth of my prayer and preaching, yet in my doctrine through all these opinions, pleading the contrary, yea abasing my self, and exalting a Christ that then I

knew

knew not. Now after this I return'd to my wife in *Suffolk*, and wholly bent my mind to travel up & down the country, preaching for monies, which then I intended for *London*, so coming to *Colchester* where I had *John Aplewhit*, *Purkis*, and some other friends, I preached in publick; so going for *London*, a mile from *Colchester*, I set my Cane upright upon the ground, and which way it fell, that way would I go; so falling towards *Kent*, I was at a stand what I should do there, having no acquaintance, and but little money, yet whatever hardship I met withal, I was resolved for *Gravesend*, so with much a do I got that night to a town called *Bilrekey*, it being in the height of Summer, and in that town then having no friends, and I think but six pence, I lodged in the Church porch all night, so when day appeared, I took my journey for *Gravesend*, and in the way I spent a groat of my six pence, and the other two pence carried me over the water; so being in the town, I enquired for some strange opinionated people in the town, not in the least owning of them, but seemingly to ensnare them, which they directed me to one *Rugg* a Victualler, so coming in, though having no monies, yet I called for a pot of Ale, so after a few words uttered by me, the man was greatly taken with my sayings, in so much that he brought me some bread and cheese, with which I was refreshed, and bid me take no care, for I should want for nothing, you being the man that writ *The Pilgrimage of Saints*, I have had a great desire to see you, with some soldiers and others, so for the present he left me, and informed Cornet *Lokier* and the rest, that I was in town, who forthwith came to me, and kindly received me, and made way for me to preach in the *Blockhouse*; so affecting my doctrine, they quatered me in the Officers lodging, and two days after they carried me to *Dartford*, where there I preached; so against the next Lords-day came for *Gravesend*, and there preached in the Market-place, which was such a wonder to the town and countrey, that some for love, and others for envy, came to hear, that the Priest of the town had almost none to hear him, that if the Magistrate durst, he would have apprehended me, for I boldly

boldly told them God dwelled not in the Temple made with hands, neither was any place more holy then another, proving by Scripture, that where two or three were gathered in his name, God was in the midst of them, and that every Believer was the Temple of God, as it is written, *God dwelleth with a humble and contrite spirit* ; So after this we went to *Maidston* and *Town-maulin*, and there I preached up and down, so at last having given me about five pounds, I went to my wife and promised in two weekes to return again, which I did, but I found not *Lokier* nor the rest so affectionate as before, for he had a gift of preaching,& therein did seek honor, so suspicious of my blasting his reputation, slighted and persecuted me, so that I left them, and towards *Maidston* travelled, so one *Bulfinch* of *Town-maulin* having friends towards *Canterbury*, perswaded me to go with him, and so against the next Lords-day, having no steeple free, we had a Gentlemans barn free, where a great company was assembled : then for *Sandwich* I went, and up and down found friends, so coming to *Canterbury* there was some six of this way, amongst whom was a maid of pretty knowledge, who with my Doctrine was affected, and I affected to lye with her, so that night prevailed, and satisfied my lust, afterwards the mayd was highly in love with me, and as gladly would I have been shut of her, lest some danger had ensued, so not knowing I had a wife she was in hopes to marry me, and so would have me lodge with her again, which fain I would, but durst not, then she was afraid I would deceive her, and would travel with me, but by subtilty of reason I perswaded her to have patience, while I went into *Suffolk*, and setled my occasions, then I would come and marry her, so for the present we parted, and full glad was I that I was from her delivered, so to *Maidston* I came, and having got some six pounds, returned to my wife, which a while after I went for *Kent* again, but found none of the people so zealous as formerly, so that my journey was but a small advantage to me, and then I heard the maid had been in those parts to seek me, but not hearing of me, returned home again, and not long

after

after was married to one of that ſect, and ſo there was an end
of any further progreſs into *Kent.* Then not long after I
went for *London*, and ſome while remained preaching at *Bowe*
in Mr. *Sterry's* place, and *London-ſtone*, but got nothing ; ſo
to *Suffolk* I went , and having but one childe, put it to nurſe,
intending to go to my Parents in *Lancaſhire* : So leaving my
Wife at my couſin *Andertons* , I hearing of *Seekers* in *Hart-
fordſh're*, went thither , and at laſt was hired by Mr. *Hickman*
to preach at *Peters* in *St. Albans* , ſo being liked, I was hired
for a moneth longer, ſo fetcht my Wife , and there continued
till ſuch time the Town of *Sanderidge* took me for their Miniſter, and ſetled me in the Vica idge, where Sir *John Garret*,
Colonel *Cox*, and Juſtice *Robotom* came conſtantly to hear me,
and gave me ſeveral Gifts, ſo that in heaven I was again ; for
I had a high pitch of free Grace, and mightily flown in the
ſweet Diſcoveries of God, and yet not at all knowing what
God was, onely an infinite Spirit , which when he pleaſed did
glance into his people the ſweet breathings of his Spirit ; and
therefore preached, it was not ſufficient to be a profeſſor, but
a poſſeſſor of Chriſt, the poſſeſſion of which would cauſe a
profeſſion of him, with many ſuch high flown notions , which
at that time I knew no better , nay, and in truth I ſpeak it,
there was few of the Clergy able to reach me in Doctrine or
Prayer ; yet notwithſtanding, not being an Univerſity man, I
was very often turned out of employment , that truly I ſpeak
it, I think there was not any poor ſoul ſo toſſed in judgement,
and for a poor livelihood, as then I was. Now in this my pro-
ſperity I continued not a year , but the Parſon being a ſuper-
ſtitious Cavelier, got an Order from the Aſſembly of Divines
to call me in queſtion for my Doctrine , and ſo put in a drun-
ken fellow in my room : and thus was I diſplaced from my
heaven upon earth, for I was dearly beloved of *Smiths* and
Thrales , the chief of the Pariſh. Well there was no other
way but for *London* again , and after a while ſent my Goods
for *Suffolk* by water : now at this I concluded all was a cheat,
yea preaching it ſelf, and ſo with this apprehenſion went up

and

and down *Hartfordshire*, *Bedford*, and *Buckinghamshire*, and
by my subtilty of reason got monies more or less; as of one at
Barton, I had twelve pounds for the printing of a book against
the Commonalty of *England*, impeaching them for traytors, for
suffering the Parliament their servants, to usurp over them,
judging the Common-wealth was to cut out the form, and
shape of their grievances, and send it up to their servants the
the Parliament to finish, shewing, as the Common-wealth
gave the Parliament power, so they were greater then the
Parliament, with matter to the effect. And then being presented to a small parish in *Lincolnshire*, thither I went, but
finding no society to hear, I grew weary thereof, and stayd
with some friends at *Oford*, so with a little monies went home
again, and not long after going into *Lincolnshire*, I preached in
several places, that at last Captain *Cambridge* hearing of me,
and was much affected with me, and made me teacher to their
Company, and said I should have all necessaries provided me,
and a man alowed me; then I was well recruited and horsed,
so that I judged it was the mercy of God to me, my distress
being great, and my care for my family. Now after a while our
Regiment went for *London*, so though I had preached in *Lin-
coln*, *Horncastle*, *Spilsby*, and many other places, yet they
would excuse me for two moneths, having no need of preaching at *London*, so with what monies I had I went to my wife,
and staid there a while, and so came for *London*: Now our
Reigment being *Twisltons*, Quartered in *Smith-field*, but I
Quartered in a private-house, who was a former friend of mine,
asked me if I heard not of a people called *My one flesh*? I said
no, what was their opinion, and how should I speak with any
of them? Then she directed me to *Giles Calvert*. So that now
friends, I am travelling further into the *Wilderness*, having now
done burning of Brick, I must still wander in the mountains
and deserts; so coming to *Calvert*, and making enquiry after
such a people, he was a fraid I came to betray them, but ex-
changing a few words in the height of my language, he was
much affected, and satisfied I was a friend of theirs, so he writ
me

me a Note to Mr. *Brush*, and the effect thereof was, the bearer hereof is a man of the greatest light I ever yet heard speak, and for ought I know instead of receiving of him you may receive an Angel, so to Mr. *Brush* I went, and presented this Note, which he perused, so bid me come in, and told me if I had come a little sooner, I might have seen Mr. *Copp*, who then had lately appeared in a most dreadful manner; so their being *Mary Lake*, we had some discourse, but nothing to what was in me, however they told me, if next sunday I would come to Mr. *Melis* in *Trinity-lane*, there would that day some friends meet. Now observe at this time my judgment was this, that there was no man could be free'd from sin, till he had acted that so called sin, as no sin, this a certain time had been burning within me, yet durst not reveal it to any, in that I thought none was able to receive it, and a great desire I had to make trial, whether I should be troubled or satisfied therein : so that

Seventhly, I took my progress into the *Wilderness*, and according to the day appointed, I found Mr. *Brush*, Mr. *Rawlinson*, Mr. *Goldsmith*, with *Mary Lake*, and some four more : now *Mary Lake* was the chief speaker, which in her discourse was some thing agreeable, but not so high as was in me experienced, and what I then knew with boldness declared, in so much that *Mary Lake* being blind, asked who that was that spake? *Brush* said the man that *Giles Calvert* sent to us, so with many more words I affirmed that there was no sin, but as man esteemed it sin, and therefore none can be free from sin, till in purity it be acted as no sin, for I judged that pure to me, which to a dark understanding was impure, for to the pure all things, yea all acts were pure : thus making the Scripture a writing of wax, I pleaded the words of *Paul*, *That I know and am perswaded by the Lord Jesus, that there was nothing unclean, but as man esteemed it*, unfolding that was intended all acts, as well as meats and drinks, and therefore till you can lie with all women as one woman, and not judge it sin, you can do nothing but sin: now in Scripture I found a perfection spoken of, so that I understood no man could attain perfection but this way, at

D   which

which Mr. *Rawlinson* was much taken, and *Sarah Kullin* being then present, did invite me to make trial of what I had expressed, so as I take it, after we parted, she invited me to Mr. *Wats* in *Rood-lane*, where was one or two more like her self, and as I take it, lay with me that night : now against next sunday it was noised abroad whit a rare man of knowledge was to speak at Mr. *Brushes*; at which day there was a great company of men and women, both young and old; and so from day to day increased, that now I had choice of what before I aspired after; insomuch that it came to our Officers ears ; but having got my pay I left them, and lodged in *Rood-lane*, where I had Clients many, that I was not able to answer all desires, yet none knew our actions but our selves; however I was careful with whom I had to do. This lustful principle encreased so much, that the Lord Mayor with his Officers came at midnight to take me, but knowing thereof, he was prevented. Now *Copp* was by himself with a company ranting and swearing, which I was seldom addicted to, onely proving by Scripture the truth of what I acted; and indeed *Solomons* Writings was the original of my filthy lust, supposing I might take the same liberty as he did, not then understanding his Writings was no Scripture, that I was moved to write to the world what my Principle was, so brought to publick view a Book called *The Single Eye*, so that men and women came from many parts to see my face, and hear my knowledge in these things, being restless till they were made free, as then we called it. Now I being as they said, *Captain of the Rant*, I had most of the principle women came to my lodging for knowledge, which then was called *The Head-quarters*. Now in the height of this ranting, I was made still careful for moneys for my Wife, onely my body was given to other women: so our Company encreasing, I wanted for nothing that heart could desire, but at last it became a trade so common, that all the froth and scum broke forth into the height of this wickedness, yea began to be a publick reproach, that I broke up my Quarters, and went into the countrey to my Wife, where I had by the way disciples plenty,

which

which then Major *Rainsborough*, and Doctor *Barker* was minded for Mr. *Walis* of *Elford*, so there I met them, where was no
small pleasure and delight in praising of a God that was an infinite nothing, what great and glorious things the Lord had
done, in bringing us out of bondage, to the perfect liberty of
the sons of God, and yet then the very notion of my heart was
to all manner of theft, cheat, wrong, or injury that privately
could be acted, though in tongue I professed the contrary, not
considering I brake the Law in all points (murther excepted:)
and the ground of this my judgement was, God had made all
things good, so nothing evil but as man judged it; for I apprehended there was no such thing as theft, cheat, or a lie, but
as man made it so : for if the creature had brought this world
into no propriety, as *Mine* and *Thine*, there had been no such
title as theft, cheat, or a lie; for the prevention hereof *Eve-
rard* and *Gerrard Winstanley* did dig up the Commons, that so
all might have to live of themselves, then there had been no
need of defrauding, but unity one with another, not then
knowing this was the devils kingdom, and Reason lord thereof, and that Reason was naturally enclined to love it self a-
bove any other, and to gather to it self what riches and honor
it could, that so it might bear sway over its fellow creature ;
for I made it appear to *Gerrard Winstanley* there was a self-love
and vain-glory nursed in his heart, that if possible, by digging
to have gained people to him, by which his name might become
great among the poor Commonalty of the Nation, as afterwards in him appeared a most shameful retreat from *Georges-
hill*, with a spirit of pretended universality, to become a real
Tithe-gatherer of propriety; so what by these things in others,
and the experience of my own heart; I saw all that men spake
or acted, was a lye and therefore my thought was, I had as
good cheat for something among them, and that so I might
live in prosperity with them, and not come under the lash of
the Law; for here was the thought of my heart from that saying of *Solomon*, Eccles. 3. 19. *For that which befalleth the sons
of men, befalleth beasts, even one thing befalleth them ; as the one
dieth,*

dieth, so dieth the other, yea, they have all one breath, so that a man hath no preheminence above a beast; for all is vanity, all go into one place, all are of the dust, and all turn to dust again. So that the 18th and 19th verses of *Ecclesiastes* was the rule and direction of my spirit, to eat and to drink, and to delight my soul in the labor of my minde all the days of my life, which I thought God give me as my portion, yea to rejoyce in it as the gift of God, as said that wise Head-piece *Solomon*; for this then, and ever after, till I came to hear of a Commission, was the thought of my heart, that in the grave there was no more remembrance of either joy or sorrow after. For this I conceived, as I knew not what I was before I came in being, so for ever after I should know nothing after this my being was dissolved; but even as a stream from the Ocean was distinct in it self while it was a stream, but when returned to the Ocean, was therein swallowed and become one with the Ocean; so the spirit of man while in the body, was distinct from God, but when death came it returned to God, and so became one with God, yea God it self; yet notwithstanding this, I had sometimes a relenting light in my soul, fearing this should not be so, as indeed it was contrary; but however, then a cup of Wine would wash away this doubt.

But now to return to my progress, I came for *London* again, to visit my old society; which then *Mary Midleton* of *Chelsford*, and Mrs. *Star* was deeply in love with me, so having parted with Mrs. *Midleton*, Mrs. *Star* and I went up and down the countries as man and wife, spending our time in feasting and drinking, so that Tavernes I called the house of God; and the Drawers, Messengers; and Sack, Divinity; reading in *Solomons* writings it must be so, in that it made glad the heart of God; which before, and at that time, we had several meetings of great company, and that some, no mean ones neither, where then, and at that time, they improved their liberty, where Doctor *Pagets* maid stripped her self naked, and skipped among them, but being in a Cooks shop, there was no hunger, so that I kept my self to Mrs. *Star*, pleading the lawfulness of

our

our doings as aforesaid, concluding with *Solomon* all was vanity. In the interim the Parliament had issued forth several Warrants into the hands of Church-members, which knew me not by person, but by name, so could not take me, though several times met with me, that at last the Parliament to him that could bring me before them, would give a hundred pounds, so that one *Jones* for lucre of mony, knowing me, got a Warrant to apprehend me, who meeting me in the four swans within *Bishopsgate*, told me he had a Warrant from the High Court of Parliament to take me : Let me see it, said I, you have no power to serve it without an Officer, and so would have escaped, but could not the people so thronged about me, and a great tumult there was, some fighting with him for an Informer, but being a City Trooper, and some more of his Company with him, they carried me, as I take it, to Alderman *Andrews,* where they searched my Pockets; but having dropped an Almanack that had the names of such as sold my books for me, they found it, and carried it to the Parliament, so informed the House I was taken, and likewise desired to know what they should do with me, who gave Order to bring me by water to *Whitehall-*staires, and deliver me to *Barkstead's* Soldiers, where after a while a messenger was sent to take me into custody, where I was lodged in *Whitehall* over against the *Dial,* and two souldiers guarded me night and day, for which I was to pay; but some being of my principle, they would guard me for nothing, and a Captain of theirs would give me moneys; so after two days I was sent for before the Committee of Parliament to be examined : so being called in, they asked me my Name, my Countrey, with many such frivolous things; so coming to the business in hand, Mr. *Weaver* being the Chair-man, asked me if I lodged in *Rood-lane* ? To which I answered, Once I did. Wherefore did you lodge there ? Because I had a friend there of whom I hired a chamber. What company of men and women were those that came to you ? To instance their names I cannot, but some came as they had business with me. Who were those women

in

in black Bags that came to you? As now I know not. But Mr. *Claxton*, we are informed, you have both wives and maids that lodgeth with you there? Those that informed you, let them appear face to face, for I never lay with any but my own wife. No : for you call every woman your wife? I say I lye with none but my wife, according to Law, though in the unity of the spirit, I lye with all the creation. That is your sophistication, but deal plainly before God and Man, did not you lye with none in *Rood lane*, and others places, besides your wife? I do deal plainly as you, but I being a free born subject ought not to accuse my self, in that you are to prove your charge. Mr. *Claxton* confess the truth it, will be better for you : for we assure you shall suffer no wrong. What I know is trueth, I have, and shall speak. What did you at Mrs. *Croe* in *Rederiff*? I had conference with the people. As you were preaching, you took a pipe of Tobacco, and women came and saluted you, and others above was committing Adultery. This is more then I remember? No, you will not remember any thing against you : but surely you cannot but remember this *Almanack* is yours, and these mens names your own hand writing. Yea I did write them, was not these men your disciples? They were not mine, but their own. Did not Major *Rainsborough*, and the rest lye with other women? Not as I know. But Mr. *Claxton* do you remember this book is yours? I never saw that before, but may be some of the like nature I have. Why did not you write this Book? That you are to prove. Here is the two first Letters of your name. What is that to me? it may serve for other names as well as mine. Did not Major *Rainsborough* and these men give you monies to print this Book? How should they give me monies to print that which neither I nor they knew of. This Book must be yours, for it speaks your language, suitable to your practise. I being but a stranger to you, how should you know my language or practise? Though you will confess nothing, yet we have witness to prove it. Let them be examined in my presence : So calling *Jones* hat betrayed me, did you never see Mr. *Claxton* lye with no wo-
                                                                              man?

man? I have heard him tal of fuch things, but faw no act.
Though you cannot, there is fome will, oherefore Mr. *Clax-*
ton deal plainly, that though you lay with none, yet did not
you alow it none others? I faw no evil in them to difalow;
And Gentlemen let me fpeak freely to you, Suppofe I were
your fervant, entrufted with your fecrets, and knew that you
were Traitors againft this prefent Power, would you take it
well for me to impeach you, and bear witnefs againft you? At
which, either the Earl of *Denby*, or the Earl of *Salisbury* faid,
No: Such a fervant deferved to be hang'd; at which they
laughed and faid, this was a cafe of another nature. I fay as it
is in the one, fo it is in the other. Well then, Mr. *Claxton*, you
will not confefs the trueth. You fay you have witnefs to
prove it. However the trueth I have confeff'd, and no more
can be expected. Do not you know one *Copp*? Yea I know
him, and that is all, for I have not feen him above two or three
times. Then they faid, this is a fad principle, which if not routed, all honeft men will have their wives deluded. One of them
faid, he feared not his wife fhe was too old, fo they difmiffed
me to the place from whence I came, and faid we fhall report
it to the Houfe, that fo with fpeed you may have your trial, but
I think it was about fourteen weeks before I received the Sentence of the Houfe, which took up the Houfe a day and half
work, as *John Lilborn* faid, ftood the Nation in a Thoufand
pounds: And thus they fate fpending the Common-wealths
monies, about frivolus things. Now having paft fome votes,
at laft they carried the day for my banifhment, which vote
that day was printed, and pafted upon many pofts about the
City of *London*, *That* Lawrence Claxton *fhould remain in*
New bridwel *a moneth and a day, and then the High heriffe of*
London *to conduct him to the High Sheriffe in* Kent, *and fo to be*
banifht England, Scotland *and* Ireland, *and the Territories there-*
of during life, and Major Rainsborough *to be no longer Juftice*
during his life. Now when my moneth was expired, their
Vote was not executed, fo after a while I came forth of prifon,
and then took my journey with my wife to my houfe in *Stain-*
feild,

fi.ld, and from thence I too my progress into Cambrigdeshire, to the towns of *Foxen* and *Orwel* where still I continued my Ranting principle, with a high hand.

Now in the interim I attempted the art of Astrology and Phisick, which in a short time I gained and therewith travelled up and down Cambridgeshire and *Essex*, as *Linton* and *Saffronwalden*, and other countrey towns, improving my s ill to the utmost, that I had clients many, yet could not be therewith contended, but aspired to the art of Magick, so finding some of Doctor *Wards* and *Woolerds* Manuscripts, I improved my genius to fetch Goods back that were stoln, yea to raise spirits, and fetch treasure out of the earth, with many such diabolical actions, as a woman of *Sudbury* in *Suffolk* assisted me, pretending she could do by her witch-craft whatever she pleased; now something was done, but nothing to what I pretended, however monies I gained, and was up and down looked upon as a dangerous man, that the ignorant and religious people was afraid to come near me, yet this I may say, and speak the truth, that I have cured many desperate Diseases, and one time brought from *Glenford* to a village town wide of *Lanham* to Doctor *Clark*, two women and one man that had bewitched his daughter, who came in a frosty cold night, tormented in what then *Clerk* was a doing, and so after that his daughter was in perfect health, with many such like things, that it puffed up my spirit, and made many fools believe in me, for at that time I looked upon all was good, and God the author of all, and therefore have several times attempted to raise the devil, that so I might see what he was, but all in vain, so that I judged all was a lie, and that there was no devil at all, nor indeed no God but onely nature, for when I have perused the Scriptures I have found so much contradiction as then I conceived, that I had no faith in it at all, no more then a history, though I would talk of it, and speak from it for my own advantage, but if I had really then related my thoughts, I neither believed that *Adam* was the first Creature, but that there was a Creation before him, which world I thought was eternal, judging that land

of

of *Nod* where *Cain* took his wife, was inhabited a long time before *Cain*, not considering that *Moses* was the first Writer of Scripture, and that we were to look no further than what there was written; but I really believed no *Moses*, Prophets, Christ, or Apostles, nor no resurrection at all: for I understood that which was life in man, went into that infinite Bulk and Bigness, so called *God*, as a drop into the Ocean, and the body rotted in the grave, and for ever so to remain.

In the interim came forth a people called *Quakers*, with whom I had some discourse, from whence I discerned that they were no further than burning brick in *Egypt*, though in a more purer way than their fathers before them; also their God, their devil, and their resurrection and mine, was all one, onely they had a righteousness of the Law which I had not; which righteousness I then judged was to be destroyed, as well as my unrighteousness, and so kept on my trade of Preaching, not minding any thing after death, but as aforesaid, as also that great cheat of Astrology and Physick I practised, which not long after I was beneficed in *Merfland*, at *Terington* and St. *Johns*, and from thence went to *Snetsham* in *Norfolk*, where I was by all the Town received, and had most of their hands for the Presentation, then for *London* I went, and going to visit *Chetwood* my former acquaintance, she, with the wife of *Middleton*, related to me the two Witnesses; so having some conference with *Reeve* the prophet, and reading his Writings, I was in a trembling condition; the nature thereof you may read in the *Introduction* of that Book [*Look about you, for the devil that you fear is in you*] considering how sadly I had these many years spent my time, and that in none of these seven Churches could I finde the true God, or right devil; for indeed that is not in the least desired, onely to prate of him, and pray to him we knew not, though it is written, *It is life eternal to know the true God*, yet that none of them mindes, but from education believeth him to be an eternal, infinite Spirit, here, there, and every where; which after I was fully perswaded, that there was to be three Commissions upon this earth, to bear record to the three Titles above, and that this was the

last

laſt of thoſe three : upon the belief of this I came to the know-ledge of the two Seeds , by which I knew the nature and form of the true God, and the right devil , which in all my travels through the ſeven Chuches I could never finde , in that now I ſee, it was onely from the revelation of this Commiſſion to make it known.

Now being at my Journeys end, as in point of notional wor-ſhip, I came to ſee the vaſt difference of Faith from Reaſon, which before I conclude, you ſhall hear , and how that from Faiths royal Prerogative all its ſeed in *Adam* was ſaved, and all Reaſon in the fallen Angel was damned, from whence I came to know my election and pardon of all my former tranſgreſſions ; after which my revelation growing, moved me to publiſh to the world, what my Father was, where he liveth, and the glory of his houſe, as is confirmed by my writings now in publick ; ſo that now I can ſay, of all my formal righteouſ-neſs, and profeſſed wickedneſs, I am ſtripped naked, and in room thereof clothed with innocency of life , perfect aſſu-rance, and ſeed of diſcerning with the ſpirit of revelation . I ſhall proceed to anſwer ſome Objections that may be raiſed, as unto what I have already aſſerted.

Firſt, *What had become of me if I had died before I heard of this ſpiritual laſt Commiſſion ?*

Anſw. I infallibly againſt angels and men, that is, againſt all the ſeed of Reaſon whatſoever, declare, That if I had dy-ed in my time of wickedneſs, I had been damned. But then, you may ſay , How can this can be that I ſhould have been damned then, and not now, when the determinate will of God ſtands ſure, *that who before of old ordained to condemnation*, or ſalvation, ſo ſhall election ſtand. As unto this, it is to be ſe-riouſly minded, that while I was travelling through *Egypt* , or the wilderneſs, I knew no more than *Paul* when he was a blaſ-phemer, that I was elected as I do now , and at that time had no perfect peace, nor fully perſwaded of my ſalvation at all ; for alas, what comfort is it to a man that is ready to be turned over the ladder, and knoweth of no pardon , no more than a man that dieth in ignorance knoweth his election ; ſo that you

may

may behold what a sad journey most part of the world do travel in, even betwixt hope and despair; for it is unpossible that a soul in unbelief should know whether he be elected, or no : and therefore that Determination or Decree, doth produce a means to effect the end of that mans salvation, springing in the Well of Faith, the knowledge of his election, with a protection or preservation of its own seed from the breach of the Law; or if that soul have transgressed the Law, he shall not die till a Commission come in being; so that I being elected, and yet having broken the Law, there was a necessity I should live till this last came in being, for the Law would have condemned me, and God would have disowned me, so that there was no other way but the belief of this Commission, to free me from the law of sin and death, into eternal life.

But you may say, *What became of all the Seed of Faith since the Apostles to this day, that had not a Commission to believe in, and lived in wickedness as I have done?*

As unto this I say, all the seed of *Adam* that lived till capable of a Law, did not commit wickedness, but was kept innocent from breaking the Law ; which innocency of life, though not knowing any other, but Jesus Christ the Son of God, shall be raised to glory. For this is to be understood, that till within these thirty years, there hath no angels sounded above the Baptist, and therefore no such provocation to tempt the Seed of Faith to commit sin, as hath been in my days ; for the sixth angel sounding forth, the Ranting principle broke forth all maner of wickedness with a high hand, that did tempt such as I to break the Law as themselves : So that I say, the Seed of Faith that was not to live till this Commission came in being, had no such provocation, there being no such tempting Dispensations then apparent as they are now, so that they were all kept innocent in their lives from committing of sin, [minde this] not from thinking or speaking, but from acting sin, without which act the Law will not condemn thee ; for the Law hath nothing to do with the heart, but an act, as it is written, not he that thinketh, *but he that committeth sin, is of the devil* ; therefore blame not my revelation that it frees you

E 2 from

from looks or thoughts upon a woman, but rather rejoyce eſcaping the act, [otherways none] no not the Seed of Faith would be free from ſin, and then how will you blot out that ſaying, 1 *John* 3. 9. *Whoſoever is born of God doth not commit ſin, for his ſeed remaineth in him, and he cannot ſin* ; and all the account is given, *becauſe he is born of God.* Then in the firſt of *John* 1.8. *if we ſay we have no ſin we deceive our ſelves, and the truth is not in us,* ſhall your blinde learned Reaſon that never ſpake this, or ſhall I in the height of revelation of the ſame Seed interpret this ? that he that is born of God, as I am now, cannot ſin to act ; but if I, that am according to birth, of the Royal Seed, ſhould ſay I have no motion to ſin, I ſhould be a liar like unto the ſeed of Reaſon : will ye believe this, or believe your lying imagination ? however for your further ſatisfaction, read the thirteenth Chapter of my *Paradiſical Dialogue* ; ſo that I ſhall return to the next *Query*, where you may ſay,

Shall all the Seed of Faith now living believe in this Commiſſion, or ſhall not the innocency of life as well ſave them now, as
when there was no Commiſsion in being ?

Anſwer. There is not any of the ſeed of Faith now living, but if he hear the report of our Commiſſion ſound in his ears, though never ſee our faces, but he will believe ; though all the ſeed of reaſon hear or read never ſo often, they cannot believe; but ſo many of the ſeed of *Adam* now living in this our day, that do not hear of us, nor ſee our writings, and ſo die in the ignorance of it, through their innocency of life, ſhall be happy on the other ſide of death, though not ſo happy here ; for this I know, the real belief of a Commiſſion, gives perfect peace and full aſſurance here, which the other wants, and therefore I infallibly ſay it is ſeven times more happy to be ſaved by a Commiſſion, then by innocency of life ; ſo that O the freedom, O the freedom that attends a Commiſſion!

Again you may ſay, may a man receive your Commiſſion with joy in the belief of it, and afterwards fall away to eternal perdition ?

Anſwer. Yea, a ſoul may come to believe the glorious per-
ſon

son of our Lord Jesus, to be the onely God, and no other infinite spirit besides him, and that he is now with the same person that was crucified, in heaven glorified ; as unto this I have known some in *London*, and elsewhere, that have rejoyced in it, and contended for it ; and yet not being rooted in the right seed, it hath in time withered and turned back to *Egypt* again. Now the main thing of such a ones falling away, in plains tearmes, is, because they are according to birth the seed of reason, which may go very far with a believer in this Commission, as *Judas* with the twelve, before it be betrayed, which at one time or another, it is found out and so condemned ; as the devil *Langly* exceeded most of you in this nature, yet not believing a prerogative, fell off and despised, for which, is now eternally damned.

Again one thing more is required to be *answered*, whether one that hath received the truth in the power and love thereof, whether such a real believer, may be left over to break the law? and if, how delivered?

Answer. As unto this I say, a Commission changeth not the nature of man, but according as he was in unbelief subject to passion, wanton carriage, or foolish language, and such like, [as is too much apparent in some] will now and then be tempting that soul sutable to its nature to disturb its present peace, through the fragments of reasons nature that hangs about him; but as to action in breach of the law, a Commission doth change the power of corruption, that though he is not free from motions to sin, yet he is freed from the act of sin, this I finde in my own soul the truth of what I write, but whether an elected vessel in the real belief of this may once slip into act, as Adultery and such like, and by returning with faith in the Commission may be recovered, this I cannot gain-say but it may be so, as I could instance: but let it be a warning to all others hereafter, and remember I told thee so.

Secondly, *whether ever any, let him be of what Church soever, had a Call, or were sent by voice of words, but a Commission onely?*

Answer. As I am endued with the height of revelation, that neither angel nor man can take from me, which revelation

hath

hath begot most of you into the belief of this Commission,
let me tell you that I write not now as I have done formerly,
when I was in *Egypt* or the *Wilderness*, but I write infalibly,
without the help of any, as it flows by inspiration or revelation
from my Royal seed-spring, otherways it were no other but reasons imagination, and so it may be true or it may be false, as
all your Philosophical Histories are dubious to the writter, and
indeed the Reader thereof doth approve of no other language,
but what is written with a provisio, under correction to better
judgements, and more learned Fathers, and so like a School-
boy that writes by direction of his Tutor, so do ye write the
Commissioners revelation and form of worship contained in
Moses, the Prophets, and Apostles, and not from any revelation of your own, though you write you have a call from God, &
are sent of God, when you shall hear to the contrary; as suffer
me but to instance the vain deceit and judgling carriage of the
Quakers, in their pretended Errands and Messages to Kings
and Rulers of this kingdom, publishing they are sent of God,
to tell them, that for their pride, their vain-glory, oppression,
and cruelty, they shall have their kingdom rent from them, as
it was from *Oliver* before them; with these and such like
delusion their souls are possest withal, that they are sent, and
by the Lord commanded, when in the revelation from my
seed-spring I know they are liars, as in these particulars shall
appear:

First, That God did never speak to any of you, as he spake to
Moses, *Paul*, and *John Reeve*, if you can deal plainly, and tell
me if ever Christ from the Throne of glory, did ever audibly
to the hearing of the ear, say: *George Fox*, *Francis Howgil*,
or *John Harwood*, or any of you, behold I send you forth as my
onely true and last Messenger to the King of *England*, or any
other, to reprove them of sin whatsoever, and therefore ye go
beyond the seas to other Nations, saying the Lord sent you,
when from that spirit of divine voyce that spake to *John Reeve*
I tell you, you go forth in the strength of Reasons lying imagination, which you call your light within you, and so receive
the reward of your deceit upon you, as in the day of account
you

you fhall know that you run before you were fent.

Secondly, Do but obferve the nature and form of words you deliver, are they any other but borrowed from the Prophets and Apoftles, and fo ye run up and down with their Commiffion, and their Doctrine, repeating what they faid to Kings and Rulers, who were truly and really fent forth to deliver what they fpake: now you in the vertue of anothers Commiffion, bufie your felves like the feven fons of *one Sceva a* Jew, *who were vagabonds exorcifts, that took upon them to call over them which had evil fpirits, in the name of the Lord Jefus, faying, we adjure you by Jefus whom* Paul preacheth; So ye *Baptifts, Ranters,* but efpecially the *Quakers* like vagabonds run with the letter and doctrine of *Mofes,* the Prophets and Apoftles, faying, *Hear this I pray you, ye heads of the houfe of* Jacob, *and princes of* Ifrael, *that abhor judgement and pervert all equity, they build up* Sion *with blood, and* Jerufalem *with iniquity, the heads thereof judge for reward, the Priefts thereof teach for hire, and the Prophets thereof divine for money, and yet they will lean upon the Lord, and fay, is not the Lord among us, none evil can come unto us?* With thefe and fuch like fayings ye go to the Magiftrate and Miniftery, and bid them remember what judgements the Prophets threatned againft fuch Magiftrates and Minifters, not in the leaft having any call or command from God in your felves, without doubt and confidence, faying, I *George Fox* by vertue of my Commiffion that was given by voyce of words from the mouth of the Lord Jefus in the higheft heavens, do infallibly againft Angels and Men, tell thee O King, the Parliament, and Clergy of *England,* if ye eftablifh fuperftition, and bind mens confciences to your form of worfhip, then know this O King, that the God that bid me tell thee, contrary to thy expectation, will rayfe up an Army againft thee, that will blaft the proceedings of thee and thy Councel for ever, I fay were ye thus called, and fent forth, as ye were true Meffengers, fo would your Meffage take effect, and prove true as ye have publifhed.

But poor blind Creatures! as really & truly as I know Chrift Jefus the onely God, and the Prophets and Apoftles commiffioned, missioned, and sent forth by God, so I as really believe ye neither know God, nor were sent forth by God, but are meer dissemblers, and liars against the true Commissioners of God; therefore I tell thee O King, and all powers under thee, that this last Commission of the eternal spirit, hath no Messages to Kings or Rulers touching the Affairs of their Government, and therefore as we have none, (thou shalt not need to credit any other,) onely this by permission I say, if thou so far retain the Prerogative in thy own hand, that no Councel, Bishop, or Minister, may molest or persecute any Opinion, Church, or Dispensation, much our Commission, that is contrary to them in matter of worship, provided they be obedient to thy Government in just civil things, I say, if this be really performed by thee, thou and thy posterity, after thee may in safety reign during this perishing world: This being done, let him be of what Church soever, that shall not without Hipocrysi of heart, be free from writing or fighting against thee, be punished.

Now ye being false, and not sent, notwithstanding all your woes, plagues, and judgements you threaten against a Kingdom (if they do but repent) though they punish with death, they be happy as well as you, not knowing your own happiness, you cannot discern anothers (when it is not so in ours) you having no discerning of the two seeds, *viz.* Faith and Reason, you make no differences, but wraps up all together, not knowing but Gods nature, Reason and Mans the same, and so if man do but hearken to the light of Reason within him, he shall be as happy as the Seed of Faith, *and thus ye are blind leaders of the blind*, pretending a Call, and sent of God, and yet you know not the form of God, nor his nature, thinking that in *Adam* both Seeds die, and so in Christ both shall be made alive, not at all that Reason was damned in the Angelical Serpent, and Faith saved in *Adam*, as in the *Quakers Downfal*, and the *Dialogue* is opened at large.

Now had you been Commissionated by voice of words, or were it possible to think of an inward Commission by the Spirit, as some of your fine-spun Professors do imagine, and to me

was

was confirmed by one *Laine*, but especially by one *Tomlinson* a very moderate Brother of yours, that would prove a Call from God, so sent of God by the succession of the Spirit, not understanding that the Apostles, who were the Stewards and Shepherds of Christ, and in his stead had the power of salvation and condemnation committed to them, were all put to death, with every Believer of them : then how do you think they, being the conduct of the Spirit, that you should receive the influence of their Authority from a dead letter, and that conveyed to you by the Roman power that put the true Commissioners to death, it is like there should be a succession, either by voice of words, or the Spirit, when you have neither of them both, but the light or learning of Reasons imaginations onely.

And then, if ye had a Commission by voice of words, so sent of God, your language and your worship would speak for you, that you were the true and last Messenger of the third and last Commission ; but alas, poor deluded creatures, you are the last angel that ever shall sound a pretended truth, yet real lying notion that ever shall appear in this world; concerning which both the Ministers and Hearers are ignorant, that the Teachers of the *Quakers* are the last angel spoken of in the tenth of *Revelation*, the seventh verse, saying, *In the days of the voice of the seventh angel, when he shall begin to sound, the mystery of God should be finished, &c.* Now ye angels or teachers of the *Quakers*, do ye send forth any other doctrine or worship, but what is recorded in the Commission of others, even what they said, and did do, as near as you can do ye; which if ye had a discerning spirit, you would without censure or envy, read our revelation flowing from a Commission, doth far transcend the language or worship of either of the two Commissions before us ; but ye being of the angels nature, so the seed of the Serpent, ye know not the voice of a Commission from a Dispensation : As touching which, I shall open in the third Objection or Query, thus stated.

Whether there ever was more then one truth at a time, and whether there be more than one way to this truth ? and if but one way,

F   *which*

which is the true and onely way to the truth.

Answer. Truth was never known till a Commissioner was chosen, so that till *Moses* there was nothing made manifest what was truth, and what not, and therefore from thence it must be enquired, whether there was more then one truth, he being the first writer of truth that ever was, doth all along tell you in his days, there was but one truth, the knowledge of which consisted in the true God, as in the first Command it is written, *thou shalt have no other Gods before me*, so that this was the onely true God; and therefore saith *Moses*, *there is none like unto the Lord our God*: and again it is written, *thou art the God, even thou alone*; and so all along the Prophets do declare no other God, but what before by *Moses* was revealed, crying, *I am God, and there is none else, I am God, and there is none like me, therefore look unto me, for I am God, and there is none besides me.*

Then, and at that time, this was truth, yea the onely truth, and no truth besides it, though then most part of the world worshipped idols, yea a lie of their own invention, yet in the Commission of *Moses* was truth onely maintained, under the title of God the Father.

Secondly, After this God became flesh, as it is written, *The word was with God, yea the word was God, which word was made flesh, and dwelt amongst men*, now called a Son, or Christ the Savior, which none but the Apostles Commission believed, as from their saying, *there is no other name under heaven given among men whereby we must be saved*, with many sayings to that purpose, proving that Christ was the Son of God.

Then, and at that time, this was truth, yea the onely truth, and no truth besides it, though then there were both Saducees and Pharisees, yea most part of the Jews, and almost all the Gentiles worshipped a God besides Christ, yet in the Commission of the Apostles, was truth onely revealed under the title of Christ the Son.

Thirdly, After this, yea in this instant time, both Father and Son are in this our third and last Commission made manifest to be the holy Ghost, or one entire spiritual body, yea the same

body,

body, and no other body but what upon the cross suffered, is now in heaven glorified, both Father and Son, one spiritual form, Creator of heaven and earth, so called the Lord Jesus.

Now, and at this time, this is the truth, yea the onely truth, and no truth besides it, though all the Seven Churches pretends to know truth, and so by their professions holds forth seven truths, yet I infalibly say in this our last Commission, this is the truth onely revealed under the title of Christ, as he is a spiritual person not in us, but above us, in his own kingdom of glory, blessed for ever.

And yet they are not three truths, but one truth, as in respect of God the Father, God the Son, and God the holy Ghost, which three are not persons, but titles comprehended in the single person of Christ alone; but as in relation to their Commissions in time, they are three Commissions, in three distinct persons, though they all three acknowledge themselves to have their authority from one and the same person; for that person which spake to *Moses*, spake to *Paul*, and spake to *John Reeve*: the truth of this is clearly revealed in my *Dialogue*, the second and twelfth chapters, so that I shall omit to speake any further, onely leave you to that saying of *Paul*, *he that descended, is the same also that ascended*, so that still it is but one, and the same person, even Jesus alone, but:

Secondly, As there is but one truth, so there is but one way to this truth, and that must needs flow from them that are the publishers of truth; for it is ridiculous to think that man or men which knowes not truth, should be the way of truth, [therefore take notice and do not forget,] as there is no truth but in a Commission, so there is none, let them be never so wise or eloquent, yea righteous, or heaven-like, if he be not a Commissioner sent by voyce of words, and that audibly to the hearing of the ears, from the spirit of divine faith that cannot lie, I tell thee thou art no shepherd, but an hireling; no son, but a bastard; no true Commissioner, but a counterfeit: as deal plainly, can any of you the Angels or Teachers of the seven Churches, infalibly say, that God by voyce of words, sent you as he did *Moses*, the Apostles, and *John Reeve*? certain I am

without

without doubt ye cannot. O then what do you think will be the end of all your profound lies, that you have preached in publick and private, by taking upon you succeſſively to be Prophets, Apoſtles, and Miniſters from anothers Authority, and thereby you cavel and rayle one brother againſt another, ſaying the Papiſt, Eſpiſcopal, Presbyterian, and Independent, are falſe Prophets and hirelings, and they ſay, you Baptiſts, Ranters, and Quakers are falſe Prophets and deluders, and who ſhall be judge of your pretended Commiſſions, and railing accuſations, ſhall the Scripture that is a dead letter? or ſhall I that have the ſpirit of revelation? can any of you tell me, who made you Miniſters and Teachers over others? the Apoſtles and their Biſhops diſowns you, their writings ſay your fathers murthered all of them, ſo that there was not one left alive to continue their ſucceſſion, by impoſition of hands or otherways, ſo that what can you ſay for your ſelves, but that the Pope, who was made the ſupream head over the dead letter, and that Roman power eſtabliſhing it, by its ſupream authority, you have your ordination from Miniſters, and from no other God or ſpirit, but the dead letter onely: now let me tell you all, and yet not I, but the ſpirit of revelation, flowing from my ſeed-ſpring, [mind what I ſay,] that I am as truely ſent now, as *Timothy* and *Titus* were in their Commiſſion, and therefore I can without fear, and with a real undoubted confidence ſay, that you are all but the Meſſengers of Men, and therefore the next time ye read or preach from the tenth of *John*, remember that you read your ſelves the falſe Prophets and Hirelings there quoted, as in the day of eternal account you ſhall finde the truth of what I ſay, but then too late, and in vain will your doleful cries be.

But you may object and ſay from thoſe words of Chriſt, ſaying, *I am the good ſhepherd, and know my ſheep, and am known of mine*, from hence you may cavel, and ſay there is no mortal man a true ſhepherd, but Chriſt alone, and that becauſe he ſaith, *I am the way, and the truth, and the life.*

Anſwer. I grant that Chriſt is the great ſhepherd of the ſheep, and was the onely Prophet then living, yea then and at
                                                                that

that time, he was the onely way to eternal life, and all that believed in him were his sheep and followed him, for then the
Apostles were but sheep, and Christ their shepherd, but after
that our Lord and good shepherd, had by his blood purchased
eternal happiness for his sheep, then he Commissionated his
Apostles to be shepherds in his place, as before he was ascended
he bid Peter *feed his sheep*, which after they were indued with
power from on high, they went forth in the strength of their
Commission, and declared themselves to be Ambassadors and
Stewards in Christs stead, yea the way and life of their salvation; and therefore saith Paul, *bretheren be followers togcther of
me*, knowing assuredly if they believed in their Doctrine,
they should be as happy, as when they believed the words of
Christ from his own mouth, so that this know there is no going
to God, but by Commissioners, for who they curse are cursed,
and who they bless are blessed, in that the revelation thereof
hath an infallible discerning who are the seed of *Adam*, and
who are the seed of the Serpent.

And therefore take notice if Christ be the way now, and
teacheth you by his spirit, why are you not therewith contented, and keep every man at home, but run up and down the
City, some to publick and some to private, neglecting waiting
upon God, and teachings of his spirits, to wait upon men and
their vain teaching? and so the priests tells them they must
wait upon God, in the use of means, imitating a true authority saying the Lord sent them, when they neither know the Lord
nor their Message, so being but mans Ministers, they compel
men to go the broad way with them to destruction.

4. Again, you read but of two ways, a true and a false, the
narrow way, and the broad way, that is, the way of Faith, and
the way of Reason, so unless you deny Scripture, you cannot
but confess, that as truth is onely in a Commission, so then
of necessity it must follow, that the true Commissioners are
the narrow way, and way of Faith to eternal Truth. So that
ye seven Churches what do you say for your selves? are you
right, or are you wrong? are you true, or are you false? Sure
I am you do all say, that you are in the truth, and the ways of
truth:

truth: if ye will not believe me, enquire of *Moses* and the A-
poftles, and fee if they do not fay that there was no truth but
in a Commiffion, and ask them if truth were ever eftablifhed
by Authority ? [minde this] fure I am you will finde it recorded, that truth was onely contained in one Commiffion to another, and that truth was ever perfecuted by Authority. Have
you not read this ? do ye not believe this ? then from the letter I fhall prove this, that the hypocritical *Scribes and Phari-
fees did build the tombs of the Prophets , and garnifh the fepul-
chres of the righteous, and fay, if we had been in the days of our
fathers , we would not have been partakers with them in the blood
of the Prophets* : So your fathers murthered Chrift and all his
Apoftles, and fince their children have eftablifhed the Ordinance of the Apoftles, and with tradition and learned Philo-
fophy, have garnifhed the letter of the Scriptures with a penal-
ty, that if any one do fpeak againft *Moses*, Chrift, or the Apoftles, they fhall be punifhed; fo that ye be witneffes unto
your felves that you feven Churches are the onely heires of
them that killed the Apoftles.

As now the laft and higheft truth is held forth in this our
laft Commiffion, as in my writings I have told you again and
again, that there is no truth but what is revealed by us, and
no way to eternal happinefs without us, fo that when you have
eftablifhed that fo called *Religion* I then expect no other dea-
lings at your hands, than our brethren the Apoftles found
from your fore-Fathers ; and then your fons in the next gene-
ration, will fay of you as now ye fay of your fathers ; but wo,
wo, if not for fear, yet for fhame leave off your tearming your
felves the Churches of Chrift, and that your traditioned notional Forms are the true ways of Chrift, that fo you may be more
excufable in the eternal Account of the Lord. Do but enquire whether the way of *Moses* and the Prophets be your rule
now, when it was not the Apoftles in their time? and fhall
you that belong neither to *Moses*, nor the Apoftles, by fuccef-
fion of voice of words, or infpiration of the fpirit, ordain your
felves Bifhops and Minifters by the dead letter of the Apoftles, and then you fetch your garb and attire from the dead
                                                            letter

letter of *Moses*? all which was abolished in the death of Christ, [and by the Apostles detested against as beggarly rudiments] so no examples for any mortals now living to imitate, [minde that] unless you do wilfully shut your eyes against what the Apostles say, and what I now write ; for the glory of this perishing world hath so bewitched you to believe a lye, that you wrest the Scripture into an image of wax, framing it according to Reasons imagination, your onely idol, god, and savior, when from an infallible spirit I say, there is not one sentence in the letter of Scripture to warrant any of you seven Churches in your Forms of Worship, nor can you from any grounds of reason make *England* believe that you are the true Bishops and Ministers of God, unless you could make it apparent that you were all Jewes, and all the world besides you Heathen Gentiles, that worshipped gods of stocks and stones, then you might have some colour to practise the Rites and Ceremonies of the Law; which if you could, you must not onely wear *Aarons* holy garments, but your male, both yong and old, must be circumcised, and have your peace-offerings and burnt-offerings of the blood of bulls and goats, with all other Ceremonies thereunto belonging, that so the ignorant might have some faith in you ; but in that most of your Churches knows that the Jews and the Gentiles are by mixture of seeds become one Nation, they can tell you there was no Bishops, Elders, or Deacons in *Moses* or the Prophets time, and therefore ye pretending a succession from *Timothy* and *Titus*, your younger brethren, *viz.* Presbyterian and Independent, *&c.* can inform you, if ye were true Bishops, in stead of the holy garments of *Aaron*, you must with *Timothy* and *Titus* wear a mean garb, as plain habit, and such like, and not to go with long Gowns and Sircingles; and in stead of variety of Dainties, you must eat with no gentile, but suffer want and hunger ; and in stead of a Coach and six horses, you must go on foot ; yea, in room of many Attendance to serve and wait upon you, you must wait and serve your flock : if you had believed Scripture, as ye pretend to make it your rule, why do ye not imitate the true and great Bishop Christ Jesus? who saith, he that is the greatest.

est, and will bear rule, must be a servant to others, saying, though I be the son of God, nay God himself, yet I washed my disciples feet, and there was no room for me in an Inn, but a manger, and I never ride but once, and that was upon an Ass, thus was I humbled, and abased my self; and though ye pretend a Commission successively, yet ye altogether exalt and honor your selves, in contempt of me and my true Commissioners; So that as I am the true and onely Bishop now living, seeing ye boast of things that was *Moses* and the Apostles labors, and like School-boys, vaunt your tongues in other mens rules of things made ready to your hands, [minde what I say] yet whether ye do or not, I infallibly tell you from that spirit of divine voice, in the person of the Lord Jesus, that spake to *Moses*, *Paul*, and *John Reeve*, that you have now no goard to shadow you from that dreadful sentence of this our spiritual and last Commission of the most high and mighty God, the Man *Jesus*.

Now having sufficiently shewen ou, that all Churches, Dispensations, Gifts, or Ways are false, not] proceeding from a Commission, and that from a Commission then in force and being; but all the seven Sons, or Churches, have all proceeded from no Commission, but from Reasons invention to establish others revelations for their rule: so now I shall shew you in a few particulars, that ye all run in vain, and so do lose the prize of the high calling, the knowledge of the Man *Jesus*.

First, in that ye know not who he is, nor where he is, that ye run to, and therefore some of you run after a God of three persons, when you have neither Scripture nor revelation for to warrant you the truth of your journey; and others of you run after a God of an infinite Spirit and two persons; and the rest of you run after a God that hath no person at all, so that I say you are all out of the way, and really believes no God at all, neither can any of you say with *Paul, I know in whom I have believed*; but ye run doubtfully, not being fully perswaded that the God ye preach and pray to, is the true God, neither indeed do ye trouble your selves to know what he is, but onely
speak

speak the word Father, the word God, the word Christ Jesus,
as a tradition educated by your fore-fathers, established in
your Articles, Creeds, and Catechisms, exercising your disciples from them to believe as the Church believes, not having
faith in any thing ye profess : As deal plainly and impartially,
answer me upon your salvation, as you hope to see your God
in glory, that you are fully perswaded, that your God and your
devil is the way, and the truth, and no other besides it ? I say
not any of you can avouch it as the principle of your assurance,
that the God ye profess is the true God, and yet what a rabble
rout of pretended believers there is among you, that some of
your members swears, God damn them they believe in God,
be drunk, and believe in God; whore, and believe in God;
cheat, and believe in God; bear false witness, and believe in
God; tyrannize and oppress, and believe in God; nay, the
Land lords for a Quarters-rent will turn the poor into the
streets, and yet believe in God; and the great devil Broker
will usurp 30 or 40 pound in the hundred, and protest he believes in God; so that I say ye have made a by-word of the
name *God*, and a very pack-horse of the Scriptures to seal up
your own damnations; as when I was among you, this was
my condition, and the state of you all, in one of those evils or
another; so that with admiration, against angel or man I can
say, I have not run in vain, that those which in the knowledge
of God I thought was before me, are all left behinde zealous
in their devotions to the unknown God whom ye ignorantly
worship, which in all my writings I have revealed, that your
God cannot be known neither to Saint or Angel, having no
form or person, but an infinite eternal Spirit without a body,
how do you think your nothing God should be known ? nay,
had *Abraham* known no other God than ye profess, he had
never been tempted to slay his son, in that from such a God
there had been no invitation, neither had his confidence been
so far fixed, as to obey a command without a body; but he
really believing that his God was no shadow, but a personal
substance, made *Abraham* so willing to offer up his onely beloved son *Isaac*. Now your faith having no foundation to

G   pitch

pitch its confidence upon, but as in a Lottery men venture their money, so do ye in your worſhip venture your ſalvation, not really knowing at all that your preaching and praying is to a true God, onely ye hope well, yea hope the beſt, that you are in the truth and the right way, and that your God is the God, when I infalibly tell you he that runneth to God, or profeſſeth God *muſt believe him as he is*, [O mind what you read] not as he is in your hope, and vain imagination, but as he is really in himſelf, a glorious perſonall God : and know this while you are in hope you do not believe, *for hope that is ſeen is not hope, for what a man ſeeth, why doth he yet hope for?* thou knowing God is true as thou believes, hope is ſwallowed up in that belief, *for the hope of the hypocrite ſhall periſh,* but when thou canſt without doubt ſay as *John* ſaid, we hope not, *but we believe, and really know that we are of God, and the whole world lieth in wickedneſs, and we know that the Son of God is come, and hath given us an underſtanding, that we may know him that is true, and we are in him that is true, even in his Son Jeſus Chriſt, this is the true God and eternal life,* once come to this, thy hope is no more hope, but becomes faith.

Which I am certain there is not any of you the ſeven Churches, that knowes the true God, and the right devil, the true heaven, and right hell, no without doubt I know that all your hopes, ſo living and ſo dying, that hath been acquainted with our Commiſſion, ſhall eternally periſh : and furthermore I know, that if ye did believe *Moſes*, Chriſt, and the Apoſtles, ye would believe me, I knowing that ſo many of you as really believes the two former Commiſſions, if ye hear but our report, will as really believe in us, though I know all of you will ſay, ye believe in *Moſes*, Chriſt, and the Apoſtles, but ye cannot believe in us : And why do ye not underſtand we are the laſt Commiſſion, as they the firſt and ſecond ? even nothing but becauſe ye know us alive, and by tradition are educated to believe them though dead ; for while Chriſt and the Apoſtles was among them, they were of no more eſteem than we. As to this purpoſe, ſaith *Paul, His letters* [ſay they] *are weighty and powerful, but his bodily preſence is weak, and his ſpeech con-*
temptible,

temptible, so while any living knows our persons, for that our writings are despised; however, let me resolve you why you cannot believe our words now living, is because ye are of the feed of unbelief, reason, the devil, and take this for truth, ye do not believe *Moses*, Christ, nor the Apostles; ye hope ye do, ye say ye do, as the Jewes said of CHRIST, *We are Moses Disciples, we know that God spake unto Moses, as for this fellow we know not from whence he is.* Who would have thought but what they said, was truth; yet Christ tells them *John* 5.45. *Had ye believed* Moses, *ye would have believed me, for he wrote of me, but if ye believe not his writings, how should ye believe my words?* So that from the Lord of Glory I say, did ye really believe the writings of *Moses*, Christ and the Apostles, ye would believe in our words; but I know ye do not believe, but only confess and profess for your own honor and advantage, which in the hour of death ye will be all at a loss what will become of your souls, for all your preaching and praying to your God on your bed of sickness, you have all your work to do, so that it is evident, you are all out of the way, yea still in *Egypt* or the *Wilderness.*

Fifthly, Again ye run in vain, not knowing the Scriptures; for as they were written by men, inspired with the spirit of revelation, so none can give any true interpretation thereof, but those endued with the same spirit, and that I really believe none of you can with safety say ye are the men, I certainly knowing, that your learning is from the seed of Reason, which is the wisdom of flesh; So that it is unpossible ye should discern the plain language of Faith, or give a true interpretation of Scripture written by the seed of Faith, and therefore ye know not what Scripture is, and what not, though I acknowledge your wisdom of Reason, can translate Hebrew, Greek, and Latine into English, and this being done, ye make your ignorant disciples believe that you have interpreted the Scripture, when I know that the Scripture in its divine sence, is as a ridle not unfolded unto all the learned Rabbies of the world; furthermore I can with confidence say, that when any of you do assume an interpretation, you dare not conclude that is the true

meaning

meaning thereof, and no other , and yet such of you who are
of a contrary seed to the Writers of Scripure , do take upon
you to be Judge of their writings , when I say, as I said before, you underſtand not what you are your ſelves , nor what
will become of another , neither doth the wiſdom of Faith
that ſearcheth the high things , yea the deep things of God,
proceed from the learned education of Univerſities, ſo no ſpiritual men to judge of things concerning God , and his kingdom ; O then why will ye preſume to ſay this or that is blaſ-
phemy, when you know not what God nor his nature is , the
devil or his nature is, and yet none ſo forward to cry down
thoſe that are truly ſent, for falſe prophets , deluders, back-
ſliders, and blaſphemers, when now I infallibly know that you
onely are the men ; as do but look back to the true and falſe
prophets of old , and then if you can [ſpeak the truth] that
whether the true be more in number than the falſe. *Elijah*
ſaith, [*I even I*] *onely remain a Prophet of the Lord* , *but* Baals
prieſts are four hundred and fifty men. And ſo all along in the
ſecond Commiſſion there was a great number of falſe, to the
ſmall number of true : As now in our days what multitudes
there is of falſe prophets and falſe teachers , to one true prophet and true Biſhop ? for this you muſt grant , that if ye all
be true, then *Moſes*, the Apoſtles and we, are falſe, and if ſo,
in vain were that ſaying of Chriſt , *Strait is the gate* , *and narrow is the way that leadeth unto life*, *and few* (not multitudes)
but few there be that finde it ; which if ye were all true prophets, or true teachers, [as if any of you were , it muſt be the
Baptiſt] but in that I know ye are all falſe , blot out that ſaying of our Lord, and write it thus, [wide is the gate, and broad
is the way that leadeth unto life and ſalvation , and moſt of
the world do finde it :] were it thus, ye might have ſome colour of juſtification that ye were all true, and our Commiſſion
onely falſe , then heaven would be full , and hell would be
empty. But let me tell you once more, and ſo many as are
elected will believe me , that this is the laſt Commiſſion, yea
the ſtrait gate, and narrow way, yea the onely way to eternal life, ſo narrow that no hypocrite can enter among us,

but

but he is discovered and condemned by us.

And then because it is written, *Beware of false Prophets which come to you in sheeps clothing, but inwardly are ravening wolves.* What a noise do ye make in your pulpits, one brother impeaching another for false Prophets , when I know not any of you can without doubt say, which of you are true, and which are false , though it is said , *By their fruits ye shall know them.* Can you tell me the fruits of a true Prophet from a false one ? Sure I am ye cannot ; therefore I shall tell you , how ye shall know a true from a false, [mind what you read] the fruits of a false Prophet , is to go before he be sent, yea sent by voice of words from Christ the true Ordainer of Prophets , so that ye go forth by the voice and ordination of men , so preach the doctrine of men , and that onely for your honor and preferment , this is a false Prophet, and the fruits of your prophecy, is to be chosen by your members , to fight with the sword of steel , to inrich your selves in the ruine of your disciples , to Lord it over your hearers, to teach a false God, and a false devil , to cheat and murther one another , as now ye do at this day, this all of you are guilty of , in one kind or another , and yet ye that are the onely false Prophets , say to your deluded members, these are dangerous times , take heed of false prophets ; which if ye could discern truth, ye should bid them beware of you, that they pin not their salvation upon your doctrine ; for the fruits thereof are as aforesaid , onely Reasons philosophy and vain deceit : as if you did but observe what you read, when you say , *not many wise men after the flesh, not many mighty , not many noble ; but God hath chosen the foolish things to confound the wise , and weak things of the world to confound the mighty , and base things of the world, and things which are despised, God hath chosen ; yea, and things which are not , to bring to nought things that are.* Do you believe this ? what do ye say to this ? are ye fools, are ye ignorant, are ye weak, are ye base, are ye despised ? then you might have some plea that you are the true Churches of Christ; but you are too wise, too strong, too many, too honorable to be true Bishops and Messengers of Christ the Lord of Gory , and yet you will not be-

lieve

lieve this, but perswade your selves that the richest, the proudest, and the wisest are the onely true Believers, when I infallibly know from that Spirit of divine Faith, that ye are all the sons and daughters of *Cain*, that proud *Lucifer* your father, which ere long shill have your wages with him in flames of eternal burning, and that for ever.

6. Again, you are false, and run in vain, not discerning the two seeds how they became two where they remain, with the effects and operations since the beginning to this day; but having in the fifth chapter of my *Wonder of Wonders* spoken something of this secret, I shall forbear, and in a higher nature make manifest what hath been their effects and operations, from that to this day. As unto this, all that do not willfully shut their eyes, may read as they run, that according to the saying of God, hath ever since *been at enmity*, and that not onely in its own soul, but one man with another, otherways what need had there been of a Law given to Reason the *devil*, but that Reason oppresseth and injureth another, and so makes work for the *Lawyer*, yea ever since hath devoured and murthered one another, that Reason hath erected *Magistrates*, *Judges* and *Lawyers* to reconcile Reason divided against it self, or else condemn it to be executed by the *Hangman*. That you may in brief see the fruits, and influence of Faith and Reason, I shall demonstrate what their operations are, both in spirituals and temporals.

First, As unto spirituals, both Faith and Reason do motion forth to their original, from whence they had their being, and therefore Faith in the Commission of this last age, can tell what it was before it became mortal, and what it is now being mortal, and what it shall be when immortalized again, when as Reason motion out to the same, but having by its disobedience lost its purity, and now in mortality it soars, if possible, to know what it was, what it is now, and what it shall be hereafter, but cannot attain it, in that the Covenant or promise was not made to Reason but Faith onely. As do but enquire whether *Abraham* was the father of Faith or Reason, and then you shall read *he was the father of the faithful*; and upon that

account

account the Covenant was made, with *Abraham*, as it is written, *I will establish my Covenant between thee and me, and thy seed*
after thee, &c. So that *Paul* a man of his seed saith , *Now to*
Abraham, and his seed were the promises made, &c. So that in
all the genealogy of Faith, it hath in one measure or another,
been capable of its descent, though never so clear , as now in
this last witness of the spirit, for I can with confidence say, that
my Faith hath motioned through the grave , yea pierced the
heavens , and beheld the glorious person of our Lord Jesus,
(and in that view) hath been filled full of divine revelation,
that now at its pleasure can ascend and descend in full per-
swasion, that what by Faith I have seen in glory above , I have
in part made known to you below ; for my Faith hath eviden-
ced in my soul , that what I have written as touching *God, De-*
vil, Heaven, Hell, with the death and resurrection of the soul,
is the truth and no other, without the knowledge of which no
soul can have perfect peace here , or glory hereafter ; for the
operations of Reason and Faith are much different , in that
Reason desires things impossible : for what Faith can and will
do, Reason never desires it , but is continually tempting our
Lord to impossivities, as to imagine God created the world of
nothing, and God a Spirit without body , and created the angels bodiless spirits, and that God never created man to damn
him. Now Faith knows that earth and water was eternal, and
God hath a spiritual body, and the angels likewise , and that
he created the angels Reason to be damned , so that what is
possible to Faith , is impossible to Reason, and what Reason
imagines is possible, Faith knows is possible : not but Faith can
do what it pleaseth, yet will not be moved at Reasons pleasure , but what ever Faith demands, is possible for God to do ,
in that Faith desires nothing but what is his royal pleasure, being moved in the operation of its own seed , without doubt
believing what ever Faith asketh, it shall receive, not that Faith
is boundless , but limited to its original , and so the effects
thereof is moved to demand possibilities suitable to the tenor
of its Commission , given by that divine voice of all powerful
Faith , which now is all spiritual , not moved to any external
miracles,

miracles, as the two former were, and therefore generated
Faith in all Commissions did never request Christ its Father,
but what grew in its seed possible, knowing that his prerogative
would no more move his divine will thereunto; now Reason
not knowing the mind of our God, it cries and desires that
God would send fire from heaven, and blast the proceeding of
its enemies, supposing the will of God is the same now, as it
was then, and that it is as possible for God to turn the inten-
tions of their adversaries upon their own head as formerly. I
acknowledge our God can do what his divine soul pleaseth,
yet what he hath decreed to the contrary is unpossible, and
sure I am as unto your request, *his hand is shortned,* and *his ear
heavy, that he will not hear you*; for your hands are full of blood,
your lips have spoken lies, nor have you done justice or equity
when the power was in your hands; so that in the highest pitch
of revelation I tell you, that it is a work of as great a wonder
for our God to take notice of none of you, as when he did observe all the transactions of his Commissioners before you, and
sure I am as unto externals he doth not hear us his last Commissioners, then how do ye think ye being sinners, our God
should hear you? So that I infallibly say, our Lord will not
perserve you, nor destroy you, but Reason subtilty must deliver you, as it hath delivered your enemies into your hands
before you. If ye will not believe me, then believe the fruits
of your own prayers, and much good may they do you. Answer to this, Reason flies unto Scripture, where it is written,
*I am the Lord, I change not: and Christ is the same yesterday, to
day, and for ever,* not in the least understanding the drift of
those sayings, nor believing our God in every Commission hath
new tearms of mercies and Judgements, suitable to the nature
of the Commission; for this know, those sayings lay in point
of his eternal prerogative as unto damnation, and salvation,
he is the same and changeth not: but in externals, *it repented
the Lord he made man; and repented that he had made* Saul
King; but he never repented that he saved Faith and damned
Reason, though Reason moderate can soar high with exellent
heaven-like words, if possible, with tears to move the Lord to
　　　　　　　　　　　　　　　　　　　　　　　answer

answer his desires, yet all that Reason can do, can not change our Lords prerogative, to take off that eternal curse that was given to Reason in the womb of *Eve*, it being impossible for God to do Faith never requests it, though what lies in the account of Faith nothing is impossible; as *Luke* 1. 13. that saying was spoke upon as great a work of Faith as ever was, though to Reason it is impossible that the power of the highest, which was the Father, could as swift as thought descend into the womb of *Mary*, and there dissolve into seed, and conceive himself into a mortal childe of flesh, blood, and bone, so called *Emanuel* or Jesus the Son of God, now what the royal will of all Faith had decreed and promised to do, that Reason cannot believe, but what Faith hath decreed, he will not, so cannot do that Reason would have him to do, as to make of stones bread, or come down from the Cross and save himself, which Christ could not do, because for that end he came to die that thereby he might not onely raise himself to glory, but all his seed that Reason murthered, to glory with him, and keep Reason under eternal misery; and yet how highly is Reason reputed by you, and Faith slighted with you; and that because Faith revealeth that which Reason cannot comprehend, when as Reason can declare nothing as touching eternity, but Faith can fathom it, and binde Reason hand and foot in the interpretation of it; and therefore in Scripture it is written the high transcendent vertues of Faith, but no applause of Reason at all as concerning the kingdom of God: But

Secondly, As it is the Lord and Governor of this world, so the elder brother, its products in the affairs thereof are so wise, gallant, maiestical, and glorious, that if Faith knew it not, it would delude the seed of eternity; for its wisdom is so great, that it dives into all the secrets of nature, which way to make it self happy in this its kingdom; and therefore out of Reasons seed hath sprung or risen the knowledge of all Arts and Sciences, men graving, carving, and framing, all gold, silver, brass, steel, iron, pewter, lead, glass, woollen, linnen, leather, and what not, into variety of forms and fashions, for its eye

H   to to behold, its back to clothe, and belly to feed, so that in brief there is nothing that the wisdom or hand of man hath invented, but it came from Reasons subtilty, without the assistance of Faith at all; for Faith is so ignorant and simple in the Arts and Sciences of this world, that without Reasons direction it could not make use of what Reason brings to his hand, so when Reason is moderated and well qualified, Faith hath a helpful Hindmaid of Reason, but when Reason is immoderate and hypocritical, as seldom it is otherways, O what a monster it is to Faith, that it tramples innocency under foot! yea, brands it guilty of that which onely belongs to it self, and that because Faith cannot dissemble as Reason doth; nay, immoderate Reason is so proud and majestical, that it will not suffer its moderate brother to live by it, but sue it, imprison it, and beggar it. O what a changeable, desiring, unsatisfied seed is Reason, that it is never better but when it is plotting mischief, by back-biting, envying, and if possible, to murther what it hates! So that where Faith is supream, it reigns as a Kingly Prerogative over Reason, otherways Reason would not submit; for both Seeds cannot reign, but there must be divisions till one of them be silent, not but that the conquered will scout forth upon the borders of the Law, but being captivated it cannot act, it may talk and prate what it would do, but Faith being lord, it must have license from Faith before it can conceive its thought to action; so that where Reason is lord, its operations are never satisfied, no not a year, a moneth, or a day, but inventing new fashions, new delights, new mischiefs, sometimes it will be ruled over, and sometimes it will rule it self, as these late transactions will confirm what is written, so that well may the imagination thereof be compared to a bottomless pit, for indeed it knows not what it would be, nor what it would have, never long contented, but either too full or too empty, too rich or too poor, too wise or too foolish, too high or too low; but however the true nature of Reasons motion is to be rich and great in this its heaven, for I know this world was given to Reason, with all the riches and glory

there-

thereunto belonging, and therefore let not the devil think
that this world will hold as long as it hath done, nor that it
shall enjoy its pleasure and lordly reign here, and in our kingdom on the other side of death too; for I know this is your
inheritance by birth-right, and not the Saints at all, and therefore we the last Commissioners, or the Believers thereof, shall
not plot or conspire against no Power then reigning, but submit to you however you deal with us; for it is none but your
seed that disturbs your peace; therefore Faith will be quiet
under thy reign, and pay according to our ability what is your
demand, onely in spirituals it will not spare to reveal truth in
obedience to eternity: and therefore we desire nothing of you
but what *Moses* the first Commissioner requested of *Sibon* king
of the *Amorites* in naturals, so we would have the same in
spirituals; which was, that he might but onely pass thorough
their land, not turning into their fields or vineyards, neither
would they drink their water, or eat their bread, but what they
paid for; yet the children of *Esau*, the seed of Reason, would
not let the Seed of Faith pass by, for which they in their own
kingdom were destroyed. So as I am the true and beloved
Bishop of the Lord, we request but onely to pass quietly tho-
row your kingdom, as we have not, so we will not turn to the
right, or to the left, to molest you, but be silent under your
Government: but if ye will not let us pass, but stay us in prison, and there murther us for pretended blasphemy, as the children of *Esau* would have done to *Moses* and his people for rebellion, then take notice, as sure as the *Amorites* were eternally destroyed, so shall ye be eternally damned; for to our
kingdom we must go, and without death we cannot go: but if
ye be made instrumental to hasten our journey, thereby you
hasten your misery, and remember in the height of revelation
I told ye so.

Seventhly and lastly, ye run in vain, not knowing what the
soul is, and so are ignorant what dies' and therefore by authority in my revelation I shall with all brevity that may be, make it
appear, that immortallity cannot inhabit in mortality, but one

must

muſt be ſwallowed up of the other; However ye cannot underſtand this, yet from an infallible ſpirit I know, that the
ſpirit, ſoul, and body, is all one, though three titles, yet but one
eſſence, the ſpirit mortal, the ſoul mortal, and the body mortal, yet not three mortals, but one mortal; none divine, but
all humane; for they are ſo interwoven in the blood, through
the whole body, as it is written, *the life of the fleſh is in the blood,*
ſo not two but one; that if you hang one, you muſt hang both.
As now you that ſuppoſeth the ſoul cannot die, and were
ſpectators of thoſe that were hanged, drawn, and Quatered,
deal plainly and tell me, when you ſaw their bodies by a halter
ſtifled, and by the Executioner opened, what did you ſee?
Was there any thing whipt out when the hang man came?
Certain I am, if the ſoul were immortal and could not be killed,
you would have ſeen it fly ſome whither: And this know, if the
ſoul could not die, it would not ſuffer its body to die, but take
it along with it, in that the ſoul cannot live without the body, no more than the body can live without the ſoul. O blinde
Reaſon! that you ſhould imagine you ſaw any thing but their
ſouls murthered and burned in the fire; for if the ſoul be in the
blood, (then minde) in letting out the blood, you pour out the
ſoul, as when by the ſpear there came out water and blood,
then was the ſoul of our Lord poured forth, as it is written,
he hath poured out his ſoul unto death. Now without a Scripture you will not believe that the ſoul is in the blood, and in ſpil-
ling the blood you ſpill the ſoul, then read *Jer.* 2. 34. and there
you ſhall finde, *In thy skirts is found the blood of the ſouls of the*
poor innocents; ſo that without you kill the ſoul, you cannot
kill the body, for as long as the ſoul is alive, the body is not
dead; but when the ſoul, that is the life, is killed, then the body is killed likewiſe. But then how ſhall we do with that ſaying *Fear not them which kill the body, but are not able to kill the*
ſoul, &c. the true meaning is, why the body is ſaid to be killed
and not the ſoul, in that the ſoul ſhall riſe again, and not the
body: the ſoul by death is but changed to a new life, when as
the body is killed to an everlaſting death; ſo that in relation

to

to eternity, the body is ſaid to be killed , and not the ſoul , in that the ſoul ſhall quickly riſe to life again , and bring with it a body ſuitable to its nature, as it is written , *and to every ſeed its own body* ; concerning this you may finde more at large in the ninth chapter of my *Dialogue.*

But then you will query, *If the ſoul and body be one , ſo but one life, and that life in the blood , then it is the ſoul is afflicted with pain, ſorrow, and grief, nay it is the ſoul that is faint, weary, hungry, and ſuffers cold.*

Anſw. Were ye not of the contrary ſeed, I ſhould not need to trouble my pen any further, but anſwer you in plain tearms, that it is the ſoul that eats and drinks, and that is capable of any pain, ſorrow, or joy ; nay I infallibly ſay , that when you get a childe you get a ſoul , as it is written , *And all the ſoules they had gotten, ſhe bare unto* Jacob, *ſixteen ſouls , and all the ſouls went with* Jacob *into* Egypt. *And what ſoul ſoever eateth any maner of blood: And ſhe was in bitterneſs of ſoul : his ſoul within him ſhall mourn : and my ſoul is heavy unto death.* Now theſe ſouls that were got, and upon their feet did go, and eat, and drink, *&c.* were they not men and women ? judge ye; So that now let any ſober man judge, whether that any thing but life is capable of death. O how ſenceleſs it is to think that death muſt die, and that mortal life can get to immortal life without death ! for death is the way to a new life. O then remember when you ſee a man dead, you ſee a ſoul dead, and that not verbally, but really ; for as darkneſs is as real as the light , ſo death is as real a being as life, though death is not to be under-ſtood but by life, and ſo to be owned by every true Believer.

FINIS.

An EPISTLE left upon Record for the Believers of this Commission in *London*.

BRethren, you are not ignorant that I was as one born without a *Mother*, and like a prodigal run from his *Father*, yet when I was in the height of my rebellion, my *Father* remembred me, and spread the skirts of his love over me, yea as a brand out of the fire delivered me, and in due time, by his great beloved and last Commissioner, was ordained, and in the Authority of his Commission, often related what a glorious instrument I should be, to illustrate and beautifie his Commission, the like never should come after me, with many infallible expressions uttered to our beloved *Frances* concerning me, all which was done when I was in my infancy, yet according to his revelation have proved true, as is now upon record in publick by me : O what love was bestowed upon me, that I, yea I, that was the greatest of sinners, should have the first and last fruits of his ordination, who had the voice of God, yea was spoken unto mouth to mouth by God, which none now living never had, nor never shall have like unto *John Reeve*, but onely visions, dreames, and dark speeches, which is nothing in comparison of him, yet by this the greatest Prophet that ever shall be, was I made worthy to be a fellow laborer in the work of the Lord with him, who hath not been slothful, but improved my talent beyond all now living, or that shall come after me, in discerning of hypocrites

pocrites from sound hearts, and finding out the lost
sheep of this last age, yet in all this I glory not, but
rejoyce that in my knowledge I am not puffed up, but
humble as a servant in obedience to it, for which I
slighted a good name, with the prosperity of this world,
and do stand with my life in my hand, against all spiritual Principalities and Powers of the devil: am I not
ready to offer the death of my soul, to what Reason
shall demand, that by my revelation you may hold out
to the end, and raign in glory with me, though suffer
nothing like unto me. O then can you look abroad,
and not see at home? can you be true, if I be false? can
you be happy, and I perish? Is Christ divided, that
you are at emnity? Then in vain is your Faith, have
I not labored to beget ye Sons in the truth, though
not all of you here, yet most of you elsewhere have
been the travel of my soul, to leave a Legacy behind
me, for the comfort of believers after me, which then
will be prized, though not as it ought by you regarded.
If I complain, it is because of you, that useth the freedom of a Commission in the abuse of it, I therefore in-
treat you, if ye believe it, and truly know it, be wise,
yet innocent in this your profession, and walk worthy
of it, for I am pressed in my spirit as a refiner to try
you, and sift you as corn is sifted in a sieve, and who
shall deliver you, or feed you with fancies that shall
perish with you? O brethren, let me leave this in
charge with you, and forget not what I say in mortal-
lity, lest ye be forgotten in immortallity, that you accuse
not another of that you are guilty of your selves, but
first examine at home, and then you may the better dif-
cern abroad, for from the highest to the lowest, while
im-

in mortality there will be infirmities ; O then be silent, and cover each others nakedness , and in love strengthen one another , (you are but few) and have many enemies, therefore be friendly among your selves, be kind, comfort, and that not grudginly, but willingly refresh one another, and grieve not the heart of him that hath rejoyced yours, whose soul doth mourn in love to this Commission. Are ye saints? Then banish spiritual pride, partiality, and vain-glory. Are ye believers, then revile not when reviled , see and not see , hear and not hear, do not say and unsay , send and prove, backbite, and sowe dissentions , for Faith that woketh by love, cannot quivocate nor dissemble, but doth bear and forbear; Faith that worketh by love doth abase it self, and exalt another , yea suffereth all things. O thou *Kent* and *Cambridgshire* there is much beauty in thee , and mercy flows from thee , as also some in *London* is not behind thee , for where truth is grounded in love, it doth walk suitable to a God of love , and who is contrary minded from such turn away: now the royal seed-spring within you preserve you that ye may live in love and unity as our Lord hath practised before you, then you will not fall out by the way, but like *Abraham*, take the left or right to preserve peace here, and glory hereafter.

Farewel.